❖

From the Great Deep

CLYDE de L. RYALS

From the Great Deep

Essays on *Idylls of the King*

OHIO UNIVERSITY PRESS

FOR MORSE PECKHAM

❖

Preface

While almost no one today would deny Tennyson's lyric genius, few would allow his claim to be considered as a philosophical poet. The modern critical consensus is summed up by T. S. Eliot and Paull F. Baum: Eliot in his essay on *In Memoriam* asserts that Tennyson had "the finest ear of any English poet since Milton," and Baum in his book *Tennyson Sixty Years After* finds him "disappointing as an intelligence." Yet in his own time Tennyson was considered by many—Browning, Tyndall, Gladstone, Maurice, Jowett, to name only those eminent Victorians who come readily to mind—as a man and poet whose intellectual capability was to be respected. Even the detractors among his contemporaries would never have agreed with Auden that he was the stupidest English poet.

By examining the *Idylls of the King*, I hope in this book to demonstrate some of the complexity of Tennyson's thought. I make no claim for him as a systematic thinker. I do, however, suggest that *Idylls of the King* be considered as a philosophical poem. It is not a purely philosophical poem because Tennyson was always an artist first and a philosopher afterwards. The poet was, we have it on excellent testimony, fully aware of the cultural cross currents at work in the nineteenth century. Indeed he seems to have understood the movements of thought in the period almost as well as anyone. We should not forget what—as Miss Joanna Richardson records in her recent biography of Tennyson, *The Pre-Eminent Victorian*—Huxley said to Tyndall about the Laureate: that he was "the first poet since Lucretius who has understood the drift of science."

Idylls of the King is a very complex poem, although because of the technical virtuosity and a certain surface prettiness many readers are beguiled into thinking it a simple one. Written over a number of years, it has embedded within it much of Tennyson's most mature thought. In the chapters that follow I have tried to point out some of his ideas and show how they are worked out in the poem. I am quite sure that I have not discovered all the major themes of the *Idylls*. I have hoped only to suggest that the *Idylls* is worthy of further study.

For my texts of Tennyson's poems I have used the Cambridge Edition, edited by W. J. Rolfe (New York, 1898); *Unpublished Early Poems,* edited by Sir Charles Tennyson (London, 1931); and *The Devil and the Lady,* edited by Sir Charles Tennyson (London, 1930).

I should like to thank Sir Charles Tennyson for permission to quote from his editions of the *Unpublished Early Poems* and *The Devil and the Lady,* the Houghton Mifflin Company for leave to use the Cambridge Edition of Tennyson's poems, and The Macmillan Company for permission to cite passages from Hallam Tennyson's *Memoir.*

Contents

❖

Dates of publication of *Idylls of the King*

1842 "Morte d'Arthur"

1857 *Enid and Nimuë: The True and the False.* This was a trial
volume, of which only six copies were printed. Nimuë was
the name first given to Vivien.

1859 *Idylls of the King,* containing "Enid," "Vivien," "Elaine,"
and "Guinevere"

1862 "Dedication" to Prince Albert

1869 "The Coming of Arthur," "The Holy Grail," "Pelleas and
Ettarre," and "The Passing of Arthur," the last incorpo-
rating the "Morte d'Arthur"

1870 The original titles "Enid," "Vivien," and "Elaine" expanded
into "Geraint and Enid," "Merlin and Vivien," and
"Lancelot and Elaine"

1872 "Gareth and Lynette" and "The Last Tournament"

1873 "To the Queen"; "Geraint and Enid" divided into two
parts, each being headed "I" and "II"

1885 "Balin and Balan"

1886   Part I of "Geraint and Enid" entitled "The Marriage of Geraint"

1889   The complete series published in final order:
    "Dedication"
    "The Coming of Arthur"
    THE ROUND TABLE
      "Gareth and Lynette"
      "The Marriage of Geraint"
      "Geraint and Enid"
      "Balin and Balan"
      "Merlin and Vivien"
      "Lancelot and Elaine"
      "The Holy Grail"
      "Pelleas and Ettarre"
      "The Last Tournament"
      "Guinevere"
    "The Passing of Arthur"
    "To the Queen"

❖

From the Great Deep

Tennyson and the idyll

The *Idylls of the King* have been described in many ways—as episodes, tableaux, an epic, a medley, a drama, romances, a novel, heroic poems, and romantic narratives. Yet Tennyson himself called them idylls. And to understand them we should not forget this fact. *Idylls of the King*, says J. W. Mackail in his *Lectures on Greek Poetry*, "is a title carefully chosen and significant," for Tennyson "used the name (as he used language always) with precise meaning and with a complete understanding of its Greek meaning. Here as elsewhere he showed himself not only a poet but a critic of unrivalled insight and judgment." [1]

Throughout his career Tennyson worked with the idyll, most of his best and most famous poems being in this mode. From "Mariana" through *In Memoriam* to *Idylls of the King* his poetry is characterized by an idyllic treatment. The important question to ask, then, is not whether the "English Idyls" are in fact romantic narratives or whether the

[1] J. W. Mackail, *Lectures on Greek Poetry* (London, 1910), pp. 223, 220–221.

Idylls of the King is a true epic, but, rather, why Tennyson elected to cast so large a body of his work in form of the idyll. To answer this question we must first investigate the spirit of the age which required or made possible the return to the manner of Theocritus and the Alexandrian school.

Although by now a commonplace in literary criticism, "dissociated sensibility" remains perhaps the best way of describing the dilemma of the nineteenth-century (and modern) artist. We see it in Carlyle, through the disguise of Teufelsdroeckh, when, become only the thinking man, he loses the power to feel and finds his whole self only when he discovers that it is still possible for him to feel. We see it in John Stuart Mill, who, in young manhood valuing only the analytical powers, finds himself in the "culture of the feelings." We see it in Wordsworth, who describes how he achieved a unified sensibility only when he discovered Imagination, "those sweet counsels between head and heart." We see it in Browning's *Paracelsus* and Clough's *Dipsychus*, both of which treat the polarity in modern man between intellect and emotion. In each case the whole self is realized through a bringing into proper balance of the two polar selves. This equilibrium is, however, always dynamic, always, as Faust says, seeking

> *all of life for all mankind created* [*which*]
> *Shall be within mine inmost being tested:*
> *The highest, lowest forms my soul shall borrow,*
> *Shall heap upon itself their bliss and sorrow,*

And thus, my own sole self to all their selves expanded,
I too, at last, shall with them all be stranded! [2]

The self is unstable and must always be in process of renewal. For always the problem of subjectivity, of self-immersion, presents itself: somehow an objectification, an objective embodiment of self, must continually be sought. This is, says Browning in "An Essay on Shelley," the problem of "the subjective poet of modern classification."

As explained by existential philosophers, the goal of modern man is assimilation of his experience, since only by knowing himself in relation to external reality can man know his full self. To demonstrate how this assimilation may be effected becomes one of the major themes of modern literature. This is, for example, Wordsworth's object in Book XII of *The Prelude* when he tells how a loathsome spot is transformed by its having become personalized; indeed, Wordsworth may be said to see memory as the agent by which a hateful reality is transformed into a meaningful experience. For poetry this emphasis on experience requires an actor *vis à vis* external reality to show how the object is assimilated so that subject and object, self and external reality, become one. In Coleridge's words, "a poet's heart and intellect should be *combined,* intimately combined and unified with the great appearances of nature, and not merely held in solution and loose mixture with them, in the shape

2 Part I, Scene iv, "Faust's Study," trans. Bayard Taylor (New York, n.d.), p. 94.

of formal similes." [3] Robert Langbaum, who has dealt brilliantly with the poetry of experience, says:

> The need for circumstances explains the essential situation of all poetry of experience, that the observer deliberately seeks out the experience of the poem. It also explains the unprecedented importance of nature in romantic poetry, as the most universally affecting of all circumstances—though the natural circumstance is not essential to the poetry of experience. Indeed, the success of the romanticists having turned nature into something of a *cliché*, nature poetry has since their time declined in importance. For what does matter in the poetry of experience is that the circumstance be capable of awakening fresh response, in other words that it exceed formulation. This explains the constant search of modern poetry for new settings (or at least perspectives) from which to evolve new meanings, as distinguished from the classical preference for traditional settings and meanings.[4]

Nineteenth-century poetry seeks, therefore, to achieve this end: to illuminate the inner self by describing the external object, or in other words, to talk about oneself by talking about the object. This is what Wordsworth meant in the Preface to the *Lyrical Ballads* when he said of his poems, "the feeling therein developed gives importance to the action and situation, and not the action and situation to the feeling." It is the self, the "feeling," and not the object that is important; the object is but the means by which the self is grasped and expressed. Browning, for instance, spoke to this point in the prefatory note to *Paracelsus:*

[3] *Collected Letters*, ed. E. L. Griggs (Oxford, 1956), I, 403–405.
[4] Robert Langbaum, *The Poetry of Experience* (New York, 1957), p. 50.

I have ventured to display somewhat minutely the mood itself in its rise and progress, and have suffered the agency by which it is influenced and determined to be generally discernible in its effects alone, and subordinate throughout, if not altogether excluded.

The quest of nineteenth-century poetry was for objectivity, for a means by which the self might be embodied. It was for what T. S. Eliot has called the "objective correlative," whereby emotion or feeling is presented through "a set of objects, a situation, a chain of events which shall be the formula of that *particular* emotion; such that when the external facts, which must terminate in sensory experience, are given, the emotion is immediately evoked." [5]

In his review of Tennyson's *Poems, Chiefly Lyrical* (in *The Englishman's Magazine* for August, 1831), Arthur Hallam addressed himself to the modern dilemma. "Those different powers of poetic disposition, the energies of Sensitive, of Reflective, of Passionate Emotion," he wrote,

which in former times were intermingled, and derived from mutual support an extensive empire over the feelings of men, were now restrained within separate spheres of agency. The whole system no longer worked harmoniously, and by intrinsic harmony acquired external freedom; but there arose a violent and unusual action in the several component functions, each for itself, all striving to reproduce the regular power which the whole had once enjoyed.

Hallam was of the opinion that Wordsworth had been only partially successful in his endeavor to reunify these dif-

[5] T. S. Eliot, *Selected Essays* (London, 1951), p. 145.

ferent powers. He had failed because he relied too heavily on the reflective powers in his response to experience. Those who had succeeded best, said Hallam, were Shelley and Keats, "poets of sensation rather than reflection." "So vivid [to them] was the delight attending the simple exertions of eye and ear, that it became mingled more and more with their trains of active thought, and tended to absorb their whole being into the energy of sense." Whereas Wordsworth through the medium of poetry sought understanding, the poets of sensation kept fully in mind that the business of the artist is "beauty"; they knew that "Whenever the mind of the artist suffers itself to be occupied, during its periods of creation, by any other predominant motive than the desire of beauty, the result is false in art." They were men of feeling who immediately and unpremeditatedly responded to "what is given freely," and by spontaneous apprehension of experience they were able to have a fuller apprehension than if they had apprehended only by means of the understanding. For, says Hallam,

> . . . where beauty is constantly passing before "that inward eye, which is the bliss of solitude"; where the soul seeks it as a perpetual and necessary refreshment to the sources of activity and intuition; where all the other sacred ideas of our nature, the idea of good, the idea of perfection, the idea of truth, are habitually contemplated through the medium of this predominant mood, so that they assume its colour, and are subject to its peculiar laws, there is little danger that the ruling passion of the whole mind will cease to direct its creative operations, or the energetic principle of love for the beautiful sink, even for a brief period, to the level of a mere notion in the understanding.

It is with the poets of sensation that Hallam places Tennyson. In him Hallam discerns five "excellencies," which by implication are the characteristics which a modern poet must possess. These are, in the order Hallam lists them: (1) a controlled imagination; (2) the "power of embodying himself in ideal characters, or rather moods of character, with such extreme accuracy of adjustment, that the circumstances of the narration seem to have a natural correspondence with the predominant feeling, and, as it were, to be evolved from it by assimilative force"; (3) "his vivid, picturesque delineation of objects, and the peculiar skill with which he holds all of them *fused,* to borrow a metaphor from science, in a medium of strong emotion"; (4) lyrical invention and perfection; and (5) "the elevated habits of thought, implied in these compositions, and imparting a mellow soberness of tone, more impressive, to our minds, than if the author had drawn up a set of opinions in verse, and sought to instruct the understanding rather to communicate the love of beauty to the heart." What Hallam demands of poetry, and finds in Tennyson's, is an effect of lyrical intensity, a lyrical moment in which a landscape or an episode embodies an experience. In such a poem "The tone becomes the sign of feeling; and they reciprocally suggest each other." The excellent poet, therefore, is one who has both a precise eye and a precise ear, and the perfect poem is one in which everything speaks.

In his early volumes Tennyson perfected the technique of presenting states of mind through the narrative lyric. His female characters are excellent examples. As Hallam says,

"These expressions of character are brief and coherent; nothing extraneous to the dominant fact is admitted, nothing illustrative of it, and as it were, growing out of it, is rejected. They are like summaries of mighty dramas." In "Mariana," for example, the images are all clustered around the character, and with the character serve to create a mood. The emphasis is less on the narrative than on the dramatic effect. The character is caught at a pregnant moment and the picture, which is in fact what all the poems on female characters are, emits an impression, a mood, an effect which has little to do with narrative. As Hallam saw, this is "a new species of poetry, a graft of the lyric on the dramatic." Regarded in terms of literary history, Tennyson's effort was not strictly a new species of poetry but a revival of the idyll.

Hallam was quick to anticipate the direction in which the poetry of sensation might lead. Possibly it might become so rarified that it ceased to be a means of communication. If the poet seeks to give import to the action and situation by the feeling, does this not mean, Hallam asks, "that there is a barrier between these poets and all other persons so strong and immovable, that . . . we must be themselves before we can understand them in the least?" Not so, Hallam says, because the roots of art "are in daily life and experience" and "the true poet addresses himself, in all his conceptions, to the common nature of us all." But besides this artistic consideration there is also a moral temptation, Hallam allows, in a poet's immersing himself too much in the experiences of the senses: it is dangerous for frail humanity to linger with fond attachment in the vicinity of the sense. Minds of this description are especially liable to moral temptations; and upon them, more than any, it is incumbent to remember, that their mission as men, which they share with their fellow-beings, is of infinitely higher interest than their mission as artists, which they possess by rare and exclusive privilege.

By 1830, the date of publication of *Poems, Chiefly Lyrical*, Tennyson had fully perfected the art of the idyll, "the little picture." Unless he were to repeat himself, he had to move on to something else. One way of expanding his "paintings of feelings" was to increase somewhat the narrative element and to give greater importance to outward circumstance. If we compare "Mariana" with the companion poem "Mariana in the South" of 1832, we find this is exactly what Tennyson did. As Hallam wrote to a friend about the later poem, there is "a greater lingering on the outward circumstances, and a less palpable transition of the poet into Mariana's feelings, than was the case in the former poem." [6]

A second means of expansion was to connect a series of pictures by a narrative thread. This method Tennyson essayed in "The Palace of Art," which is a poetic "Pictures at an Exhibition." The pictures are not simple descriptions; they are evocations or impressions of vistas.

> *Full of great rooms and small the palace stood,*
> *All various, each a perfect whole*
> *From living Nature, fit for every mood*
> *And change of my still soul.*

[6] Hallam Tennyson, *Alfred Lord Tennyson: A Memoir by his Son* (London, 1897), I, 501. Hereafter in this and succeeding chapters this work will be cited in the text as *Memoir*.

For some were hung with arras green and blue,
  Showing a gaudy summer-morn,
Where with puff'd cheek the belted hunter blew
  His wreathed bugle-horn.

One seem'd all dark and red—a tract of sand,
  And some one pacing there alone,
Who paced for ever in a glimmering land,
  Lit with a low large moon.

One show'd an iron coast and angry waves,
  You seem'd to hear them climb and fall
And roar rock-thwarted under bellowing caves,
  Beneath the windy wall.

And one, a full-fed river winding slow
  By herds upon an endless plain,
The ragged rims of thunder brooding low,
  With shadow-streaks of rain.

These Turneresque landscapes lose their solidity and become illuminated as perceptions. Yet they are contained within the framework of a narrative. The danger of such poetry was that the pictorial could become so important that the poem would exist simply for the sake of these beautiful paintings. Hallam had defended "Mariana in the South" by insisting that the greater lingering on the external and lesser relation to feeling was required by "the essential and distinguishing character of the conception." But, Hallam says,

Were this not implied in the subject it would be a fault: "an artist," as Alfred is wont to say, "ought to be lord of the five senses," but if he lacks the inward sense which reveals to him what is inward in the heart, he has left out the part of

Hamlet in the play. In this meaning I think the objection sometimes made to a poem, that it is too picturesque, is a just objection. . . .

(*Memoir*, I, 501)

Still a third means of enlarging the scope of the idyll was to subordinate the lyric to the narrative and insert a few descriptive vignettes here and there. Here was a chance where Tennyson could reach a wider audience and could heed the advice of friends like R. C. Trench, who told Tennyson that we cannot live in art, and F. D. Maurice, who in *The Athenaeum* in 1828 had written that a poet

cannot be a scorner, or selfish, or luxurious and sensual. He cannot be untrue, for it is high calling to interpret those universal truths which exist on earth only in the forms of his creation.

This type of idyll would draw its subject from rural life and would concern itself with unsophisticated folk and their pleasures and sorrows. In "The Miller's Daughter" and "The May Queen" Tennyson endeavored to write precisely this kind of poem.

Evidently it was in the third type of idyll that Tennyson thought himself most successful. For in the 1842 volumes almost a third of the poems approximate the genre of "The Miller's Daughter." The enlarged little picture offered a variety of opportunities: in such poems Tennyson could indulge his talent for landscape painting, could treat all classes of life, could speak out more directly on the problems of the age, and thus could engage the affections and sympa-

thies of his readers. In "Audley Court" he painted a landscape; in "The Gardener's Daughter" and "The Lord of
Burleigh" he took for subject characters from the middle
class and the nobility, and also continued to treat rural
themes in "Dora"; in "Walking to the Mail" he considered
political problems; and in "Lady Clara Vere de Vere" he
spoke of the need for human sympathy. These are the poems
which Hallam Tennyson classified as "English Idyls and
Eclogues, pictures of English home and country life, quite
original in form" (*Memoir*, I, 189). John Sterling in his review of the 1842 *Poems* (*Quarterly Review*, September, 1842)
saw in them "an epic calmness in representing some event or
situation of private life, sometimes a flow of lyrical feeling,
but still expanding itself in a narrative or description of the
persons, events, and objects that fill the poet's imagination."

Because these poems are the least acceptable of the Tennyson canon to modern taste, we are all too likely to charge
Tennyson with writing for the market place. Yet this was
not the case. For one reason, Tennyson valued his idylls as
works of art. If his aim in earlier poems had been objectification of inner awareness, in his idylls he undoubtedly thought
he was proceeding more or less along the same path. Of
"The Talking Oak," for example, a poem no one would
include in an anthology or selection of Tennyson, he told
Aubrey de Vere: "this poem was an experiment meant to
test the degree in which it is within the power of poetry to
humanize external nature" (*Memoir*, I, 509–510). In these
narrative pictures in verse, with men and women in the
foreground and nature in the background, Tennyson must

certainly have believed he had, for the time being at least, found his proper mode.

We must see Tennyson's development of the idyll as part of the general attempt on the part of poets of the first half of the nineteenth century to get poetry back in touch with life. We have only to read the Preface to the *Lyrical Ballads* and the Essay Supplementary to learn how far the poets of the beginning of the period thought poetry had passed over into the realm of pure artifice. "To what a low state knowledge of the most obvious and important phenomena had sunk," Wordsworth writes in the Essay Supplementary, "is evident from the style in which Dryden has executed a description of Night in one of his Tragedies, and Pope his translation of the celebrated moonlight scene in the 'Iliad.' "

The parallel between the first half of the nineteenth century and the Alexandrian period of Greek literature is markedly notable. Mackail says: "The Alexandrian school of the third century B. C. . . . was occupied with a single task. Its object was to get poetry back into relation with life." What poetry of the Alexandrian period had to do was to accommodate itself to a new way of life, just as poetry of the nineteenth century had to take account of new realities. Mackail continues:

> The note of the whole Alexandrian period is the emergence of the middle classes. Wealth and commerce were diffused; art was popularised; science, physical, historical, and mental, was widely cultivated. Government had passed into the hands of trained bureaucracies. Hellas had created the state and the individual, and had perished in the task. Life was thrown

back upon itself to find fresh motives and outlets. The morning-glories, the ardours of midday were over. Poetry had to find new patterns, had to attach itself as it could to a life that lay, swarming and monotonous, flat amid immense horizons, in the endless aimless afternoon.

(*Lectures on Greek Poetry*, pp. 208, 213)

It is not wholly fanciful, I believe, to consider Wordsworth as the nineteenth-century equivalent of Stesichorus, who, Mackail says, "remoulded the material of the epic under an idyllic and quasi-lyrical treatment" (p. 211). To see the truth of this comparison let us consider "Michael," which Wordsworth described as a pastoral. The pastoral had, of course, a long history in English poetry, yet Wordsworth's use of it is obviously different from that of his predecessors. "Michael" is completely without the artifice we associate with pastoral poetry, and it is free of the device whereby some sophisticated situation is enlightened by "rustic" simplicities. What I wish to say is that here we find Wordsworth, like Stesichorus, remolding previous modes and genres.

"Stesichorus himself," says Mackail, "was definitely a precursor of Theocritus" (p. 211). And likewise Wordsworth was the precursor of Tennyson. The similarity is evident when we compare Wordsworth's "Ruth" and Tennyson's "Dora." Of "Dora" Wordsworth said, "Mr. Tennyson, I have been endeavoring all my life to write a pastoral like your 'Dora' and have not succeeded" (*Memoir*, I, 265). Yet, as Matthew Arnold noted in *On Translating Homer*, Tennyson's poem is different from Wordsworth's. In comparing "Dora" with "Michael" Arnold said that "perhaps simplicity can be obtained only by a genius of which perfect simplicity is an essential characteristic." No one, to be sure, can ever claim "perfect simplicity" as an essential characteristic of Tennyson's poetry. As myriad critics have remarked, Tennyson is the poet of subtlety, learning, and sophistication.

When I say that Wordsworth was the precursor of Tennyson, I do not mean that Tennyson imitated him. I mean only to say that Wordsworth suggested a way by which modern poetry could be made more meaningful. For in Tennyson there is much of the realism of Wordsworth while at the same time there is as much "romanticism"—that is, luxuriance of expression and a tendency towards non-realistic characters. In him as in Theocritus there was, as Mackail says of the Sicilian poet, a "subtle intermixture of the two qualities."

> The return to nature took with him [Theocritus] as with his contemporaries two forms. First, it was a sustained attempt to translate the old motives, the traditional subjects, of poetry into modern terms, to re-create or re-envisage them in the surroundings of modern art, modern surroundings, a modern attitude towards life. Secondly, it was an attempt which they all to some degree shared, but which Theocritus pursued with more skill and felicity than the rest, to bring the common things of life, its occupations, studies, amusements, the middle-class range of thought and sentiment and emotion, within the sphere of poetry.
>
> (pp. 212–213)

Since we have already considered the second of these attempts on Tennyson's part, let us now turn our attention to the first—that is, the attempt to translate traditional subjects into modern terms. Tennyson in the 1832 *Poems* had looked to classic myth and Arthurian legend for subjects, and in the poems on these subjects he had tried to suggest the relevancy of this material to modern life. In "Oenone" and "The Lotus-Eaters," for example, he presented modern sentiments; and when he set about revising them, he undertook to make their modern meaning even clearer. It is with the poems on traditional subjects in the 1842 volumes, however, that Tennyson made explicit the timeliness of his matter.

Although Tennyson included the "Morte d'Arthur" among his "English Idyls," it is immediately apparent that the poem is a much different kind of idyll from "The Miller's Daughter" or "Dora." Here we have no "little picture" or lyrical character study; rather, we have an episode drawn from an heroic subject—in other words, an epyllion or epic idyll. And with its publication began what we might call the Battle between the Ancients and Moderns. Tennyson himself might be said to have begun it. For the "Morte d'Arthur," like "Godiva" and "The Day-Dream," has enclosing it a frame with a modern setting. In the frame to the "Morte," called "The Epic," Tennyson more or less debated with himself the value of a modern poet's writing on ancient subjects. Seated around the fire on Christmas Eve are a poet, a parson, a host, and a narrator. The host tells that the poet has burnt his epic in twelve books on King Arthur because

He thought that nothing new was said, or else
Something so said 'twas nothing—that a truth
Looks freshest in the fashion of the day;
God knows; he has a mint of reasons.

But, the poet asks,

Why take the style of those heroic times?
For nature brings not back the mastodon,
Nor we those times; and why should any man
Remodel models? [7]

At the end of the "Morte," purportedly the eleventh book snatched by the host from the flames, the speaker, although clearly enraptured by the poem, says: "Perhaps some modern touches here and there / Redeem'd it from the charge of nothingness." In dream the narrator sees King Arthur appear to him "like a modern gentleman / Of stateliest port." With the symbolic close the Christmas bells peal and wake the speaker. The implication is that the speaker's faith in human greatness and in legend is recovered. And having regained faith in these, he apparently is now also prepared to accept again the vitality of Christianity.

I have not done the poem justice, but I do not wish to take further space examining this poem which is not central to our concern. What I want to point out is Tennyson's use of the frame to indicate the vitality of traditional material for his own time.

The 1842 *Poems* were, generally, a critical success. I should like to examine one review of the volumes because it had, according to Tennyson himself, a profound influence on his

[7] The last line orginally read, "Remodel models rather than life?"

later development. John Sterling's critique in the *Quarterly Review,* in September, 1842, dealt in large part with the two types of idylls I have been discussing—the English idyll and the epic idyll. The English idylls were for Sterling "a real addition to our literature." "The heartfelt tenderness, the glow, the gracefulness, the strong sense, the lively painting, in many of these compositions, drawn from the heart of our actual English life," he wrote, "set them far above the glittering marvels and musical phantasms of Mr. Tennyson's mythological romances, at first sight the most striking portion of his works." Indeed, says Sterling, this is the kind of poetry a modern poet should write, a poetry which should "bewitch us with our own daily realities, and not with their unreal opposites." As for poems concerning the past and treating mythological subjects, the "Morte d'Arthur" is singled out as a poem of "less costly jewel-work" than other poems on ancient subjects "and not compensating for this inferiority by any stronger human interest. The miraculous legend of Excalibur does not come very near to us, and," Sterling maintains, "as reproduced by any modern writer, must be a mere ingenious exercise of fancy."

Although most influential, Sterling was not alone in his condemnation of legendary subjects in Tennyson's poetry. One of the points brought out by the reviewers of the 1842 *Poems* was, Shannon demonstrates in his study of Tennyson and the reviewers, that "modern poetry must idealize and mirror contemporary life and thought." [8] Poor Tenny-

[8] Edgar F. Shannon, Jr., *Tennyson and the Reviewers* (Cambridge, Mass., 1952), p. 92.

son was thus most condemned for doing the one thing he most wanted to do: to write poetry, perhaps a long poem, as "The Epic" suggests, on a subject drawn from the mythological past. Years later he told William Allingham that Sterling's review of the "Morte d'Arthur" had prevented his completing his plan for an epic in twelve books at that time.[9]

The reviewers' proscription of ancient subjects meant for Tennyson a re-examination of himself and his poetry. First, there was his well-known "passion for the past." "To me," he wrote to his future wife in 1839, "often the far-off world seems nearer than the present, for in the present is always something unreal and indistinct . . ." (*Memoir*, I, 171–172). Second, there was his belief that contemporary themes might result in a purely topical literature. In the unpublished "An Idle Rhyme," composed, Sir Charles Tennyson believes, around the time of several of his English idylls in the 1842 volumes, he wrote:

> *What's near is large to modern eyes,*
> *But disproportions fade away*
> *Lower'd in the sleepy pits where lies*
> *The dropsied Epos of the day.* [10]

Third, there was his desire to write a long poem. There survives in his son's *Memoir* a plan for an allegorical poem dating from about 1833 (II, 122). But as of the publication

---

[9] *William Allingham: A Diary*, ed. Helen Allingham and D. Radford (London, 1907), p. 150.
[10] *Unpublished Early Poems*, ed. Charles Tennyson (London, 1931), pp. 79–80.

of the 1842 *Poems* he presumably was not sure enough of his own poetic powers to undertake a long poem. He felt that "if I meant to make any mark at all, it must be by shortness, for the men before me had been so diffuse, and most of the big things except 'King Arthur' had been done" (*Memoir,* I, 166). Furthermore, "The Epic" seems to reveal his desire to write something of greater scope, especially on an Arthurian subject.

So here he was with a desire and indeed a plan for writing a long poem on the Arthurian legend. "I had it all in mind, could have done it without any trouble," his son reports him as saying.[11] "When I was twenty-four," he told Sir James Knowles, "I meant to write a whole great poem on it [Arthurian legend], and began it in the 'Morte d'Arthur.' I said I should do it in twenty years; but the Reviews stopped me." [12] What then to do? Continue in the same vein? Yet by 1842 he had already fully explored the lyric, the English idyll, dramatic monologue, and a variety of short narratives. He had made his mark by shortness. Moreover, the reviewers of the 1842 volumes had insisted that "Tennyson, if he is to establish his claim to greatness, must write a long poem—a sustained work on a single theme." [13]

So when considering a long poem, Tennyson must have reasoned more or less in this way: (1) granted a predisposition for material from the past, he would try to play up the

---

[11] Eversley Edition of *The Works of Tennyson* (London, 1907–08), III, 436.

[12] James Knowles, "Aspects of Tennyson," *The Nineteenth Century,* XXXIII (1893), 181–182.

[13] Shannon, p. 92.

contemporaneity of the subject by taking a theme and enclosing the story itself within a modern frame; (2) he would attempt to compensate for his own lack of talent for narrative [14] by breaking up the story and parceling it out to different speakers; (3) he would try to capitalize on what he knew best by blending his lyric gift with the dramatic and narrative. With such a plan he could produce a long poem by joining together a series of shorter ones. What resulted was *The Princess,* which Tennyson himself correctly described as a medley.

The Princess provided only a temporary solution, and that not wholly satisfactory, to the problem of the long poem. Tennyson's awareness of the major fault of the poem is stated in the Conclusion. "What style could suit?" the narrator asks, torn, as Tennyson was, between various demands. So he claims to be forced to move "as in a strange diagonal," with the result that the work "neither pleased myself nor them."

Examined in the light of Tennyson's previous work, *The Princess* is a series of idylls. It is, as Professor Baum has noted, "a kind of idyll on a large scale." [15] In fact, it follows the idyllic formula as previously outlined by the poet in his verse. First, there are the intercalary lyrics which are, says Mackail, idylls "completely in the Theocritean manner"

[14] Tennyson found narrative tedious. Of his difficulties in writing "Gareth and Lynette" he told Knowles: "If I were at liberty . . . to print the names of the speakers 'Gareth' and 'Lynette' over the short snip-snap of their talk, and so avoid the perpetual 'said' and its varieties, the work would be much easier" (*Memoir,* II, 113n).

[15] Paull F. Baum, *Tennyson Sixty Years After* (Chapel Hill, 1948), p. 162.

(p. 222). Secondly, there are the vignettes or descriptive idylls, which serve little dramatic or narrative purpose but apparently are included to impress upon the reader the modernity of the theme and, further, to serve the purpose of scientific observation. Take, for instance, the description of the setting and the crowd's activities in the Prologue:

> For all the sloping pasture murmur'd, sown
> With happy faces and with holiday.
> There moved the multitude, a thousand heads;
> The patient leaders of their Institute
> Taught them with facts. One rear'd a font of stone
> And drew, from butts of water on the slope,
> The fountain of the moment, playing, now
> A twisted snake, and now a rain of pearls,
> Or steep-up spout whereon the gilded ball
> Danced like a wisp; and somewhat lower down
> A man with knobs and wires and vials fired
> A cannon; Echo answer'd in her sleep
> From hollow fields; and here were telescopes
> For azure views; and there a group of girls
> In circle waited, whom the electric shock
> Dislink'd with shrieks and laughter; round the lake
> A little clock-work steamer paddling plied
> And shook the lilies; perch'd about the knolls
> A dozen angry models jetted steam;
> A pretty railway ran; a fire-balloon
> Rose gem-like up before the dusky groves
> And dropt a fairy parachute and past;
> And there thro' twenty posts of telegraph
> They flash'd a saucy message to and fro
> Between the mimic stations; so that sport
> Went hand in hand with science.

(ll. 55–80)

Here in this mixture of the pastoral and modern science we find again the Theocritean manner. Mackail says of Theocritus:

> His effort after realism issued in a form of poetry which has become the very type of unreality. But truth is that what is called realism in art is after all only a new convention; it is the essence of art that it is not nature, but an interpretation, a reconstitution of nature. The felicity of his genius is most apparent in the skill and dexterity of touch by which he gets his poetic convention into tone with the naturalistic modern touches that he incorporates with it. He even uses these so as to convey into his poetry a fresh accent of strangeness and romance.
>
> (p. 227)

These words might as well be said of Tennyson. For like Theocritus, Tennyson rarely describes just for the sake of description. In his verse, there is little "dawdling" with the "painted shell" of the universe, as Matthew Arnold seems to have thought,[16] simply for the delight of painting. On the one hand Tennyson was attempting to bring poetry into touch with life, and on the other hand he was showing that modern subjects could be used "to convey into his poetry a fresh accent of strangeness and romance." When we are told that Princess Ida and her ladies undertook a geological expedition and talked of "shale and hornblende, rag and trap and tuff, / Amygdaloid and trachyte" (III, 344-345), or when we are given such passages of description as that

16 *The Letters of Matthew Arnold to Arthur Hugh Clough*, ed. H. F. Lowry (Oxford, 1932), p. 63.

quoted above, Tennyson was but following the direction for modern poetry that Wordsworth had outlined in the Preface to the *Lyrical Ballads:*

> If the labours of men of science should ever create any material revolution, direct or indirect, in our condition, and in the impressions which we habitually receive, the poet . . . will be ready to follow the steps of the man of science, not only in those general indirect effects, but he will be at his side, carrying sensation into the midst of the science itself. The remotest discoveries of the chemist, the botanist, or mineralogist, will be as proper objects of the poet's art as any upon which it can be employed. . . . If the time should ever come when what is now called science, thus familiarized to men, shall be ready to put on, as it were, a form of flesh and blood, the poet will lend his divine spirit to aid the transfiguration, and will welcome the being thus produced, as a dear and genuine inmate of the household of man.

By 1847 the technological revolution had already progressed to the point where "what is now called science" had become familiarized, in one way or another, to men and had more or less become "a form of flesh and blood." Tennyson, whom Hallam at the beginning had classified as a poet of sensation, was thus following Wordsworth's injunction to carry sensation into the midst of science itself. As I said, he was seeking to make poetry "real" and, simultaneously, to show how romance could be found in modern life. If at the end of the Victorian period Kipling wished to show that "Romance brought up the nine-fifteen," he was but stating explicitly what Tennyson wished to do in *The Princess.*

Closely related to the descriptive idyll is what, for lack of a better term, I shall call the eclogue. This type we have met with in "Walking to the Mail." It is more narrative than descriptive, is largely conversational, and discusses matters pertinent to English national life. This may be found in both the Prologue and Conclusion. For example, "The Tory member's elder son" in speaking of France says:

> God bless the narrow sea which keeps her off,
> And keeps our Britain, whole within herself,
> A nation yet, the rulers and the ruled—
> Some sense of duty, something of a faith,
> Some reverence for the laws ourselves have made. . . .
> But yonder, whiff! there comes a sudden heat,
> The gravest citizen seems to lose his head,
> The king is scared, the soldier will not fight,
> The little boys begin to shoot and stab,
> A kingdom topples over with a shriek
> Like an old woman, and down rolls the world. . . .
>   God bless the narrow seas!
> I wish they were a whole Atlantic broad.
>
>   (Concl., ll. 51–71)

Tennyson's purpose here is that of his descriptive idyll: to bring poetry back into touch with modern life.

The third suggestion of idyll in *The Princess* may be found in the narrative itself. Here we see the depiction of domestic joy and sorrow—in the Prince's seizures, in the relationship of the Prince and Princess with their friends and parents, in the rearing of Lady Psyche's baby—and the victory of love. This type of domestic idyll may be previously found in "The Gardener's Daughter" and "Dora." Lastly, there is a hint of the epic idyll, such as was found in the "Morte d'Arthur," in the battle and in the whole epic posturizing of Princess Ida.

In *The Princess*, then, we see Tennyson attempting to meet the demands of the reviewers and to satisfy his own desires to write a long poem on a subject of contemporary importance. He did this, as I have tried briefly to demonstrate, by taking a modern theme—women's rights, treating it in terms of a subject from the past, and pointing up the relevance of his narrative by enclosing the story within a modern frame. Furthermore, he sought to overcome his lack of interest in and his lack of talent for straightforward narrative by making his story an amalgamation of idylls—lyric, descriptive, domestic, and epic.

Of the three long poems that Tennyson eventually wrote, *The Princess* alone was composed in a short period of time. Also, despite the interruptions of the intercalary lyrics and the Interlude, it is the most nearly continuous narrative of the three. It is by no means new or denigrating to say that Tennyson's genius was not conducive to the long poem as a sustained narrative. Tennyson was well aware of this limitation. He told James Knowles that "an artist is one who recognizes bounds to his work as a necessity. . . . To get the workmanship as nearly perfect as possible is the best chance for going down the stream of time. A small vessel on fine lines is likely to float further than a great raft." [17] Nor was Tennyson alone in recognizing his particular talent. In 1841 John Sterling wrote to R. C. Trench, about the 1833 *Poems* which he had been rereading, that, while he had "profound admiration of his [Tennyson's] true lyric and idyllic genius,"

[17] "Aspects of Tennyson," p. 173.

there was "more epic power in Keats." And to J. S. Mill,
Sterling wrote praising the 1842 *Poems* but adding, "There
seems a doubt whether he could conceive various character
but as a lyrical & especially a descriptive poet & writer of
eclogues he stands quite in the first class of our country-
men." [18] Tennyson's genius was for the little picture, a
lyrical moment embodying a perception and the effect of
the perception. It was this that Hallam had discerned and
praised in his review in 1831. No wonder then that Tennyson's reflections on Hallam's death took the form of various
little pictures.

Let us recall the manner of composition of *In Memoriam*.
"I did not write them," Tennyson said of his lyrics, "with
any view of weaving them into a whole, or for publication,
until I found that I had written so many" (*Memoir*, I, 304).
In the elegy itself he speaks of "breaking into song by fits"
(xxiii) and describes his lyrics as "Short swallow-flights of
song" (xlviii). Let us further recall that the trial issue run
off in the spring of 1850 bore the title "Fragments of an
Elegy."

I personally regret that Tennyson did not retain the title
of the trial issue. For "Fragments" would have given, especially to twentieth-century readers, a much better idea of
what Tennyson was about in *In Memoriam*. What he was
about was the expression of feeling, emotion, and sensibility
in terms of outward objects. He was to deal with a spiritual
problem, and his artistic problem was to extend artistic
sensibility into spiritual perception and, conversely, spir-

18 Quoted by Shannon, p. 199, n. 27.

itual perception into aesthetic sensibility. In his earlier poems he had presented diverse inner awareness in terms of diverse characters and diverse landscapes. Now he was to present one particular emotion, growing out of the experience of loss and the feelings associated with loss, in terms of, to use again Eliot's words, "a set of objects, a situation, a chain of events." But how was the set of objects and the chain of events ever to be arranged in precise logical order? Of course it was impossible. For the objects and events in his collection of lyrics had been experienced at diverse times, in diverse places, and in diverse ways, so that what he had was a series of effects.

In the late 1840's Poe in a lecture on "The Poetic Principle" had cited Tennyson as "the noblest poet that ever lived" because in him Poe had found "an elevating excitement of the Soul." A poet, Poe said in "The Philosophy of Composition," always begins "with the consideration of an *effect*," which is, we are given to understand, an effect of lyrical intensity. And since "all intense excitements are, through a psychal necessity, brief," a long poem must be "merely a succession . . . of brief poetical effects," the parts joining these effects being essentially prose.

With such a criticism Tennyson probably agreed. And when he considered the lyrics he had written on the death of Arthur Hallam he must have asked himself how his "effects" could be brought together into one poem without the necessity of "prose" linkings, how, in other words, his pictures which were united in feeling but not in logical thought could be rendered as one picture. The solution

which Tennyson adopted was a daring one and, I believe,
the first of its kind in English poetry. He would present his
fragments in logical discontinuity but would arrange them
so that the linking between the lyrics would be analogical:
the fragments would be self-contained but the connection,
the meaning, would be the work of the reader. Thus by
means of discontinuity the poem would effect the relationship of diverse "pictures." The demand on the reader would
be great. Yet as Hallam said of the new kind of poetry he
was describing in 1831:

> But this requires exertion; more or less, indeed, according to
> the difference of occasion, but always some degree of exer-
> tion. For since the emotions of the poet, during composition,
> follow a regular law of association, it follows that to accom-
> pany their progress up to all the harmonious prospect of the
> whole, and to perceive the proper dependence of every step
> on that which preceded, it is absolutely necessary *to start
> from the same point,* i. e. clearly to apprehend that leading
> sentiment of the poet's mind, by their conformity to which
> the host of suggestions are arranged.

Although many, perhaps most, of the individual lyrics
qualify as idylls, *In Memoriam* is not simply, as Mackail
describes a book of idylls, "a collection of poems on a small
scale, finely wrought and precious." In such a way the earlier
poems may be described. But if, as Mackail says, "Idyllia are
cabinet-pictures; small in size, highly finished, detachable,
not imagined and executed in any large constructive scheme"
(p. 219), then the lyrics of *In Memoriam* are not idylls at
all. I say this because the lyrics of *In Memoriam* are not
detachable. True, they are little pictures and can stand

alone, but removing a lyric violates the planned arrangement of the pictures as a whole.

To see the truth of this, let us begin with Lyric II, the first
section serving as introduction. Here the speaker sets up the
yew as a symbol of gloom but also as a symbol of stubborn
hardihood with which he will identify himself:

> And gazing on thee, sullen tree,
>   Sick for thy stubborn hardihood,
>   I seem to fail from out my blood
> And grow incorporate into thee.

Then follows the third lyric, in which Sorrow tells him that
nature is a blind thing, capricious, indifferent, and unstable.
No indication is given of the connection betwen the two
lyrics, yet to the attentive reader it is clear that III clearly
stems from II. Sorrow says, in effect: you think you can
identify yourself with a yew tree, a natural thing? Why, this
is madness, for nature is not only indifferent to your condition, it is meaningless in itself:

> 'And all the phantom, Nature, stands—
>   With all the music in her tone,
>   A hollow echo of my own,—
> A hollow form with empty hands.'

With nowhere to turn for meaning then, the speaker seeks
escape from his dilemma in Lyric IV by giving himself over
to sleep. And so it goes, each section growing out of the preceding one, although the linkages are suppressed.

In discussing the symbolist art of *In Memoriam,* which is,
as H. M. McLuhan says, the art of juxtaposing without

links,[19] I do not mean to overlook the cyclic plan of the elegy. For Tennyson's division of the poem into a seasonal cycle resulted in his fusion of the idyll, or little epic, and the cyclic epic. McLuhan says:

> In antiquity the cyclic epic of Homer and Hesiod moved away from primitive magic toward a rational and limited social function. . . . The hero task of removing the sword from the rock (as performed by Arthur and many others) is figurative of the separation of man's individual spiritual life from the collective rites of the Old Stone Age culture. Nevertheless, the cyclic epic retains the structure of the solar cycle, and from this comes its twelve- (or twenty-four-) book structure. The little epic, on the other hand, was a deliberate return to religious ritual and magic. Virgil was the first to fuse the solar or cyclic epic with the magical form of the little epic. In this fusion Virgil was followed by Dante, Milton, and Tennyson.
>
> (p. xviii)

It is important to point out the technique of *In Memoriam* because it was to have great bearing on the composition and final arrangement of *Idylls of the King*. Moreover, it was a technique Tennyson was to experiment with further in "Maud."

"Maud" is, of course, another idyll, but an extended idyll combining the various types of idyll previously identified. There is throughout an interfusion of the lyric and dramatic,

---

[19] *Alfred Lord Tennyson: Selected Poetry* (New York: Rinehart Edition, 1956), ed. H. M. McLuhan, p. xviii. I should like to acknowledge here my indebtedness to Mr. McLuhan for several ideas in this chapter.

which interfusion was the basis for the various types of idyll discerned in *The Princess*. Furthermore there is, as in *In Memoriam*, only a loose connection between the parts. In the poem, Tennyson said, "successive phases of passion in one person take the place of successive persons." [20] By centering the interest of the poem on the speaker's psychological states, however, Tennyson took attention away from the idyll as such. To many a contemporary reader it seemed a radical departure from Tennyson's previous work. He had created an audience for the little picture-poem, and when he sought to enlarge the picture, his audience ceased to recognize it as an idyll. Moreover, the picture-poem had been made almost too graphic; the attempt to get poetry back in touch with life had succeeded too well, for "life" here was not that of a pastoral setting but the life of a modern industrial society.

"Maud" was a failure with both critics and public. The other poems of the "Maud" volume, however, were received with enthusiasm. "The Brook, an Idyl" was an especial favorite. The *London Quarterly Review* of October, 1855, said tellingly: " 'The Brook' is an idyl of the kind in which Mr. Tennyson has always such success " In the *Edinburgh Review* for October, 1855, Coventry Patmore, doubtless reflecting the opinion of most of the reading public, said of it: "When we read his poetry in this kind, we wish that he might 'ever do nothing but that.' " And later in the same article Patmore went on to say, "Mr. Tennyson never wrote anything more wholesome, sweet, and real than this

[20] "Aspects of Tennyson," p. 187.

Idyl, which seems as if it had been expressly composed to refresh the spirits and restore us to a sense of life and nature after the feverish dreams of 'Maud.' " We see by these criticisms why "Maud" failed: in portraying life it had got too close to its subject; it was not the life that Tennyson's audience had been educated to look for. Here Tennyson had heeded the advice of Sterling and of such critics as the one in *The Spectator* of April 2, 1853, who had insisted that "the poet who would really fix the public attention must leave the exhausted past, and draw his subjects from matters of present import." But in the attempt he failed. Arnold had taken issue with *The Spectator* critic in his Preface to his 1853 *Poems,* and upon publication of "Maud" he wrote to Clough: Tennyson "seems in his old age to be coming to your manner in the Bothie and the Roman poem. That manner, as you know, I do not like." [21] Arnold's view was that of the majority of readers of "Maud."

The failure of "Maud" is important as background for the first *Idylls of the King.* Mr. Shannon says: "The value of chivalric lays as an antidote to the feverish dreams of 'Maud' [as Patmore characterized the poem] can scarcely have gone unrecognized by the poet, and his determination not to treat the Arthurian legend as an epic may have been influenced by these tributes to his success in the idyllic form." [22] With the first part of Mr. Shannon's statement I fully agree. Ten-

[21] *Letters to Clough,* p. 147.
[22] Edgar F. Shannon, Jr., "The Critical Reception of Tennyson's 'Maud,' " *PMLA,* LXVIII (1953). 414

nyson had wanted to write a long poem on the Arthurian
legend but had been stopped by Sterling's strictures on the
"Morte d'Arthur" and on a modern poet's treating mythological subjects. "Maud" proved, however, that a poem on a
modern subject was not necessarily acceptable. Furthermore,
the introduction by Milnes of Keats's poetry to a wider public, the work of the Pre-Raphaelites in treating medieval
subjects, and the use by both Arnold and Morris of Arthurian material had gone far towards establishing a taste
in the 1850's for mythological subject matter.

But surely it was not the failure of "Maud" which determined the non-epic treatment of the Arthurian material. As
we have seen, Tennyson in 1842 had already questioned the
viability of the epic for modern poetry. Indeed, the casting of
the "Morte d'Arthur" in the form of an epic idyll suggests a
turning away from the classical epic as a suitable form. Very
early Tennyson had doubts about the epic as the form for
his proposed long poem. Hallam Tennyson says: "Before
1840 it is evident that my father wavered between casting
the Arthurian legends into the form of an epic or into that
of a musical masque . . ." (*Memoir*, II, 124). He had been
looking for some new form, the evidence suggests; and
the success of *In Memoriam* showed that a discontinuous
arrangement of little pictures and short swallow flights of
song was more congenial not only to his genius but also to
the requirements of modern poetry. In other words, a larger
lay, in the sense of a continuous narrative, was unnecessary.

In resuming the idyllic mode of treatment of the Arthurian legend and in entitling the poem *Idylls of the King*,

Tennyson was fully cognizant of what he was about. Doubtless he had Theocritus in mind. "What Theocritus may have suggested," J. Churton Collins speculates, "was the idea of substituting a series of idylls for a continuous narrative, of composing an epic on the same principle as painters present history or biography, through a succession of frescoes painted on separate panels." [23] In the initial stages he would proceed more or less in the manner of Theocritus. Quite possibly he took as model Theocritus' three poems on Heracles, which Professor Marjorie Crump describes as follows:

> They are not in any sense epic except in dealing with epic heroes and scenes. There is no complexity or development of plot; character is either completely ignored or only indicated by the slightest touches. The epic setting gives an atmosphere of romance, but the treatment is realistic, and the purpose of the poet is to present a number of vivid pictures. The narrative is there, but it matters very little; the various incidents are successful in proportion as the reader can reconstruct the pictures more or less vividly, and through them fancy himself in that imaginary world to which the epic idyll belongs. [24]

The same words could almost be used to describe the four original *Idylls of the King*.

I mention again the resemblance to Theocritus because I want to stress how carefully Tennyson proceeded with his undertaking. Theocritus had previously proved salutary as

[23] John Churton Collins, *Illustrations of Tennyson* (London, 1891), p. 7n.
[24] M. Marjorie Crump, *The Epyllion from Theocritus to Ovid* (Oxford, 1931), pp. 66–67.

a model; indeed, it was the Theocritean manner, the Theocritean form, that had gained for Tennyson his great popularity. He would not now forsake it, as on the surface he seemed to do in "Maud," in setting forth on the composition of what he obviously envisioned as his *magnum opus.*

The modern reader is all too likely to forget how the first of the *Idylls of the King* must have seemed to a contemporary audience. It would, I believe, be beneficial if we sought to examine the four original idylls in terms of the poet's previous work, for in this way we might most nearly see the group as the audience in 1859 saw them.

First let us recall that the four idylls did not originally bear the names by which we now know them. All bore the names of women as their titles: "The Marriage of Geraint" and "Geraint and Enid" were in 1859 parts of one poem entitled "Enid"; "Merlin and Vivien" was called "Vivien"; "Lancelot and Elaine" was entitled "Elaine"; and "Guinevere" bore its present name. This point is significant, for it suggests an affinity between these poems and the earlier feminine idylls like "Dora" and "Lady Clare." Secondly, let us recall that the four original idylls, all of which were about various kinds of love, were intended to bear the collective title *The True and the False.* This fact again suggests a connection between these idylls and the earlier idylls, which in essence treated of the falseness and trueness of lovers and the consequences of their faithfulness and unfaithfulness.

I have already alluded to the many female characters in Tennyson's early poetry. At this point let us recall that these ladies have either been unfairly treated by their lovers, or have predominated over the male lover and in some way proved untrue. The *Poems, Chiefly Lyrical* of 1830 and the 1833 *Poems* offer numerous examples of these types of women: those like "Eleänore," "Rosalind," and "Lady Clara Vere de Vere," which are variations on the *femme fatale;* and those like the two "Mariana" poems and "The Lady of Shalott," which are examples of the suffering maiden.[25] Numerous poems, including those of later volumes, treat of the vicissitudes of love: "Dora" is the story of a girl who has been rejected but who nevertheless remains faithful not only to the lover but also to his family; "Oenone" treats of the maiden deserted by her lover; "Edwin Morris" tells of a lover who, because of his poverty, was not allowed to marry his beloved; "Locksley Hall" treats of the lover who lost his beloved because she deferred to her parents' wishes for a worldly marriage; "Edward Gray" recounts the misfortunes of the maiden and the lover whose marriage is opposed by the girl's parents; "Lady Clare" treats of a lover who proved true. The list is a long one and could be enlarged. It is sufficient, however, to indicate that many of Tennyson's earlier poems were about the vicissitudes of love.

My point is that the first four *Idylls of the King* most likely did not seem to an audience in 1859 as parts of any elaborate plan. I believe it highly probable that they saw these idylls simply as poems written in the same vein and

[25] See Lionel Stevenson, "The 'High-Born Maiden' Symbol in Tennyson," *PMLA*, LXIII (1948), 234–244, and my essay "The 'Fatal Woman' Symbol in Tennyson," *PMLA*, LXXIV (1959), 438–443.

approximately according to the same formula as the earlier idylls. Note that only one of the four, "Guinevere," touches directly on the main part of the Arthurian story. "Vivien," "Enid," and "Elaine" are all more or less incidental to, or even avoid, the central issues of the story. This being true, the contemporary reading public doubtless conceived and valued the first *Idylls of the King* as a group of contrasting female characters—a contrast between the true maiden (Elaine) and the true wife (Enid) on the one hand, and the harlot (Vivien) and the faithless wife (Guinevere) on the other. Seen in this light the four idylls are all based, in some way or other, on methods and formulae already familiar.

Let us look, for example, at "Enid." Geraint is sent in pursuit of a knight who has shown discourtesy to the Queen. He arrives in the knight's town without arms and goes to Earl Yniol's ruined castle to supply himself with weapons. Here he meets Enid, and here he is told that the knight whom he is pursuing has reduced her father, Yniol, to ruin. Geraint then enters the tournament against the offending knight, who as it turns out is Enid's cousin; restores the ruined Yniol to his proper station; and wins Enid as his bride. This is the part of the story which is now known as "The Marriage of Geraint." In the second part of the idyll, Geraint without reason fears that Enid is untrue to him and subjects her to all manner of insults as tests of her loyalty. Finally she proves herself, and they are happily united once again.

In this idyll, let us notice, Enid, the faithful wife, is the opposite of Guinevere; and Geraint, the husband suspicious without cause, is the exact opposite of Arthur, the deceived husband who refused to be suspicious. Enid is the suffering, almost forlorn female like the maiden in "Mariana in the South"; but she is true like Dora and the lover in "Lady Clare." She bears up under her burden and vows that

> *Far better were I laid in the dark earth . . .*
> *Than that my lord thro' me should suffer shame.*

Geraint, on the other hand, is simply an unmannerly Lord of Burleigh. This idyll is a composite of many that Tennyson wrote, and we meet with several features—the cousin-lover for example—that were characteristic of the early poems.

"Vivien" is the story of the seduction of Merlin. The portrait of the seductress draws on a number of *femmes fatales* that Tennyson had described previously. She is like Eleä-nore, a woman in whom "all passion becomes passionless"; like Fatima, who vows "I *will* possess him or will die"; like Lady Clara Vere de Vere, the "great enchantress" who seeks "to break a country heart / For pastime"; like Helen and Cleopatra in "A Dream of Fair Women," who "brought calamity" wherever they came. The only real variation on the idyllic formula that we find here is Merlin, the wise old man who is reduced to ruin by a young enchantress. But he may be regarded as an example of senile masculine weakness in contrast to the young hot-blooded passion of Geraint, or as a means of showing that while Vivien could not succeed in seducing the "blameless King," she could succeed in assotting the aged seer of Arthur's court.

The "Vivien" was also different from the other idylls in that here the veil of Victorian reticence about sexual matters was lifted for the moment to show a seduction scene. In this detail also Tennyson deviated slightly from the idyllic formula. It is perhaps indicative of Tennyson's departure from the formula that of all the 1859 idylls "Vivien" was the most seriously criticized, one reviewer sharply attacking the morality of the piece. Nevertheless, the episode was a favorite with some of Tennyson's friends: calling it "the naughty one," Jowett proclaimed it "a work of wonderful power and skill." It is also significant that this is the only one of the four poems in which readers detected a hint of allegory, what Jowett called "allegory in the distance" (*Memoir*, I, 449).

"Elaine" is of course a reworking of "The Lady of Shalott." The heroine is also one of those heroines like Oenone who have lost their lovers and have resigned themselves to humble suffering and death. Furthermore, "Elaine" is even like the earlier "Enid." There is the same situation of the rich knight riding into a strange castle and there meeting with the poor girl who falls in love with him.

I do not mean to imply that Tennyson lacked inventiveness; I am simply suggesting that he reused themes and incidents that had proved to be popular with his readers. That the theme of a maiden's unrequited love and the moral concerning faithfulness in love were popular with Tennyson's readers is indicated by this extract from a letter by Jowett: "There are hundreds and hundreds of all ages (men as well as women) who, although they have not died for love (have

no intention of doing so), will find there [in 'Elaine'] a sort
of ideal consolation of their own troubles and remembrance"
(*Memoir*, I, 449).

In "Guinevere" there is an ironic twist on the true and
false theme. Guinevere is false to Arthur but true to Lancelot. Her faith unfaithful has kept her, like Lancelot, falsely
true. She is true like Enid and false like Vivien. We find her
thus at the beginning of the idyll:

> *the Queen who sat betwixt her best*
> *Enid, and lissome Vivien, of her court*
> *The wiliest and the worst.*

Undoubtedly we are meant to see Guinevere both in likeness
and in contrast to Enid and Vivien. Her parting words to
Lancelot, "Mine is the shame, for I was wife," recall Enid's
plaintive lines, quoted previously:

> *Far better were I laid in the dark earth . . .*
> *Than that my lord thro' me should suffer shame;*

and also they recall the deceitful Vivien's hypocritical question, "for what shame in love / So love be true?"

It was, then, as a collection of female portraits that the
public in 1859 probably regarded the first *Idylls of the King*.
Each qualifies as an idyll according to Mackail's definition:
a detachable cabinet-picture. Only after additional poems
were added did the problem of form or the question of allegory arise. Readers in 1859 were not worried by either form
or allegory because, unlike later readers, they did not know

they were supposed to look for it. Of all the letters about the work printed by Hallam Tennyson in the *Memoir,* only Jowett's even hinted at an allegorical interpretation, and that of course was only "allegory in the distance."

Secondly, the 1859 readers must have realized that the four poems were about the different aspects of love, about how the true can appear false and the false true. In the very first idyll in this collection Tennyson had made a point of noting the blindness of man in this respect:

> *O purblind race of miserable men,*
> *How many among us at this very hour*
> *Do forge a life-long trouble for ourselves,*
> *By taking true for false, or false for true.*

And throughout the *Idylls* he uses the words "true" and "false" time and again. Arthur himself faced ruin because, as he tells Guinevere, "Too wholly true to dream untruth in thee," he took the false for true.

The *Idylls of the King* were immediately a success, just as Tennyson knew they would be. His confidence in the book is evident; for he had a printing of 40,000 copies made for the first edition, of which 10,000 copies were sold during the first week. The reviewers were almost unanimous in their praise; even *Blackwood's,* the magazine which had criticized him harshly in 1833, ended with this eulogy: "The pure and lofty sentiment as well as the delight furnished by these idylls will add to the debt which his country already owes to her worthy son, Alfred Tennyson." The reviewers and the buying public liked the *Idylls* because these poems were what they had come to expect of their Laureate. The *Idylls of the King* were vignettes, just as so many of his previous poems had been, which allowed the poet to indulge his genius for descriptive and short narrative verse; and even though the poems did not clearly point to any allegorical meaning, at least they had a pleasant sentiment and a discernible moral tone. Tennyson had once again captivated his audience because he apparently gave them what they expected.

Prince Albert was among those who highly valued the 1859 idylls. "They quite rekindle," he wrote to the Laureate, "the feeling with which the legends of King Arthur must have inspired the chivalry of old, whilst the graceful form in which they are presented blends those feelings with the softer tone of our present age" (*Memoir*, I, 455). Yet there were others who were of the opinion that a rekindling of medieval feeling was not the business of a modern poet. Ruskin was perhaps the most notable of these. Despite the many excellencies of the idylls, he wrote to Tennyson,

> it seems to me that so great power ought not to be spent on visions of things past but on the living present. For one hearer capable of feeling the depth of this poem I believe ten would feel a depth quite as great if the stream flowed through things nearer the hearer. And merely in the facts of modern life, not drawing-room formal life, but the far away and quite unknown growth of souls in and through any form of misery and servitude, there is an infinity of what men should be told, and none but a poet can tell. I cannot but think that the intense masterful and unerring transcript of an actuality, and the relation of a story of any real human life as a poet would watch and analyze it, would

make all men feel more or less what poetry was, as they felt what Life and Fate were in their instant workings.

This seems to me the true task of the modern poet. And I think I have seen faces, and heard voices by road and street side, which claimed or conferred as much as ever the loveliest or saddest of Camelot.

(Memoir, I, 453–454)

Such a criticism, echoing Sterling's review in 1842, must have given Tennyson pause. If these four idylls were to be made part of a larger whole, he must have felt that they should in some way be arranged so that the reader could more readily see the relationship between the poems and modern life. In the meantime, however, he would experiment with a longer idyll of the type of "Dora," in which he would concern himself directly with "life" and forget Camelot. This endeavor of course resulted in "Enoch Arden" in 1864.

But the idea of a larger group of idylls on Arthurian material would not be put down. Moreover, there was a host of people—important people like the Queen, the Princess Royal, Macaulay, and Gladstone—who wanted more of the Idylls of the King. Macaulay and the Duke of Argyll wanted an idyll on the Sangreal (Memoir, I, 456), the Princess Royal suggested joining the "Morte d'Arthur" to the four more recent Arthurian idylls (Memoir, I, 482–483). Eight years after the appearance of the four idylls the Saturday Review (November 30, 1867) expressed hope "that the Laureate himself may yet be induced or inspired to weave these noble fragments into a nobler whole. Or is it that the complete

Arthuriad is destined for ever to elude the final grasp of the Epic Muse?"

Tennyson's situation was like that of Virgil's when the Roman poet began considering a long poem. Note the similarities in this passage from Mackail's *Virgil and his Meaning to the World of To-Day:*

> Virgil was now turned forty. He had from early years contemplated the writing of an . . . epic. He had never lost sight of that design; nor had he ever for long together ceased to ponder over it, to lay plans for it, and to work at it. It now began to shape in the general scheme of the *Aeneid.* It was urged on him by the Court; it was called for by the unanimous wishes and expectations of the public; and it opened out to him the possibility of embracing in a single great masterpiece all the motives which stirred him most as a poet. It gave scope for Roman pride and Italian patriotism, for the fascination of history and archaeology, for romantic narrative, delicate psychological insight, human emotion. It enabled him to give expression to faith in the future as based on and interpreted by the past, and to his own deep thoughts on life, death, and the destiny of mankind.[26]

And Mackail's statement of Virgil's aim, "to fuse the new romantic sensibility with the epic largeness," might be applied equally well to Tennyson.

Both poets chose a picturesque subject out of their nation's half-mythological past; both sought in describing a time divided from them by dead faiths to show meaning for their own times. But in the end the two poets chose different

---

[26] J. W. Mackail, *Virgil and his Meaning to the World of To-Day* (Boston, 1922), pp. 38–39.

means to accomplish their desired ends. While employing the epyllion in various parts of his poems, Virgil imposed the structure of the cyclic epic on the *Aeneid*. Tennyson, on the other hand, was unwilling to subject his epyllia to this somewhat artificial scheme. Instead he hit upon another scheme: his idylls would follow the cycle of the year. With such a plan he could compose the individual idylls in any order he wished. Also, by means of the idyllic cycle he could fuse, somewhat in the manner of *In Memoriam,* the little epic and the solar epic.

Yet, as Mackail observes, "an idyllic cycle is not an epic" (*Lectures on Greek Poetry,* p. 223). And to treat it as an epic, or an epic *manqué,* is to regard the completed *Idylls of the King* in the wrong way. The epic is concerned with heroic action; its focus is on the hero in action. The *Idylls* does not have this as its chief concern, for Arthur is the hero in the background. Put another way, the difference between an epic and the *Idylls* is somewhat like that between Scott's and Wordsworth's verse based on mythological subjects. In a note attached to "The White Doe of Rylstone," one of Wordsworth's few attempts at embodying his conceptions in a deliberately devised mythological form, Wordsworth pointed out the difference between his and Scott's work:

> Sir Walter pursued the customary and very natural course of conducting an action, presenting various turns of fortune, to some outstanding point on which the mind might rest as a termination or catastrophe. The course I attempted to pursue is entirely different. Everything that is attempted by the principal personages in "The White Doe" fails, so far

as its object is external and substantial. So far as it is moral and spiritual it succeeds.

In describing his own poem, Wordsworth has, I think, likewise described the *Idylls of the King*. For the interest in them is always in the presence rather than the active person of the King, who, in seeking to prove himself in his knights ("Lancelot and Elaine," l. 157), fails in so far as his object is external. As Hallam Tennyson says:

> if Epic unity is looked for in the "Idylls," we find it not in the wrath of an Achilles, nor in the wanderings of an Ulysses, but in the unending war of humanity in all ages,—the worldwide war of Sense and Soul, typified in individuals, with the subtle interaction of character upon character, the central dominant figure being the pure, generous, tender, brave, human-hearted Arthur,—so that the links (with here and there symbolic accessories) which bind the "Idylls" into an artistic whole, are perhaps somewhat intricate.
>
> (*Memoir*, II, 130)

The completed cycle of the *Idylls of the King* is the consummation of Tennyson's work in the idyllic mode. If Tennyson sought by means of the little picture to find objective expression of inner awareness, in the series of enlarged pictures he hoped to implant his own private vision of life within a structure which, while exhibiting his inner perceptions, protected the vision from the ravages of its subject. For the *Idylls* are, like *In Memoriam*, fragments shored against his ruin. Tennyson knew, as Elizabeth Sewell observed in writing of Valéry, that "Words are the only defense of the mind against being possessed by thought or

dream." [27] Like his Arthur's, Tennyson's victory in the
Idylls of the King represents the control of chaos which
permits the accomplishment of his vision.

The *Idylls* are the expression of Tennyson's lifelong effort
to make a detached aesthetic impulse become fully func-
tional within an artistic form. The *Idylls* had occupied him
for many years, and from the beginning he had felt the
aesthetic impulse pull him away from a limited reality toward the region of mystic truth. By the time of the earliest
of the *Idylls*, the "Morte d'Arthur," he had already passed
beyond the struggle with aesthetic escapism as exemplified
in "The Palace of Art." His view of the world had become
enlarged, but he had not succeeded, as Sterling's review of
the 1842 volumes indicates, in giving full scope to his vision.
Like his Arthur in the beginning of the *Idylls*, he felt himself detached and lacking a tie with the temporal world.
"What happiness," Arthur asks,

> *What happiness to reign a lonely king,*
> *Vext—O ye stars that shudder over me,*
> *O earth that soundest hollow under me,*
> *Vext with waste dreams? for saving I be join'd*
> *To her that is the fairest under heaven,*
> *I seem as nothing in the mighty world,*
> *And cannot will my will nor work my work*
> *Wholly, nor make myself in mine own realm*
> *Victor and lord.*
>
> ("The Coming of Arthur," ll. 81–89)

The vision and the potential were there, but the means of
externalizing the vision was lacking.

[27] Elizabeth Sewell, *Paul Valéry* (New Haven, 1952), p. 33.

In his marriage to Guinevere and in his formation of the Round Table, Arthur found the means for expression: Guinevere becomes his bond with the temporal world and the Round Table becomes the ethical expression of his intuitive vision of a motivating spiritual power in men. Not without point does Tennyson take such elaborate care to underscore that the knights form an *order* and that for a little while they and the inhabitants move in *harmony* with the King. For the city of Camelot is, among other things, Tennyson's metaphor for poetic creation.

By a kind of magic the poet imposes a structure on fragmented experience, and his poetry becomes the re-created vision which harmonizes the disparate elements of existence. But the equilibrium, the bringing of chaotic experience into an ordered arrangement, is dynamic, as is the realization of self, and must always be in process of renewal; vision and truth must be continuously sustained by the active will. This is, I think, one of the things Merlin alludes to in his answer to Gareth's question as to whether Camelot is real or illusory:

> *For truly, as thou sayest, a fairy king*
> *And fairy queens have built the city, son;*
> *They came from out a sacred mountain-cleft*
> *Toward the sunrise, each with harp in hand,*
> *And built it to the music of their harps.*
> *And, as thou sayest, it is enchanted, son,*
> *For there is nothing in it as it seems*
> *Saving the King; tho' some there be that hold*
> *The King a shadow, and the city real.*
> *Yet take thou heed of him, for, so thou pass*

Beneath this archway, then wilt thou become
A thrall to his enchantments, for the King
Will bind thee by such vows as is a shame
A man should not be bound by, yet the which
No man can keep; but, so thou dread to swear,
Pass not beneath this gateway, but abide
Without, among the cattle of the field.
For an ye heard a music, like enow
They are building still, seeing the city is built
To music, therefore never built at all,
And therefore built for ever.

("Gareth and Lynette," ll. 254–274)

The creation is enthralling, Merlin says; and by its power of enchantment the creation meets with its greatest difficulty. For the creation demands full submission and total immersion on the part of the perceiver. In the very demands it makes, art lays the ground for its own failure: when it meets with the counterclaims of reality it suffers defeat. Even Merlin, the wisest of the inhabitants of Camelot, yields to Vivien, who, the antithesis of vision and order, seeks actively to destroy and negate the high calling of Arthur. No wonder then that lesser men cannot live up to the claims which their Order makes upon them.

In presenting the failure of Arthur's vision to recognize and re-create itself in external reality Tennyson was again using the idyllic form to embody his perceptions. For the *Idylls of the King* renders a poetic statement about a problem which belongs to the philosophy of art: the poet cannot re-create as an aesthetic entity his own vision, his own apprehension of truth. As Merlin says early in the cycle, "And truth is this to me, and that to thee" ("The Coming of

Arthur," l. 406). Merlin knows, as Arthur does not in the beginning, that in artistic creation the artist's vision cannot be wholly existent apart from its creator in the perceptions of men, the experiencers of art, unless they too have the will of the creator to experience it. But, I shall attempt to show in a later chapter, the creator cannot, as Arthur seeks to do, bind the wills of other men to himself without impinging upon the free will necessary to their apprehension of the creation.

The *Idylls* present in objective form Tennyson's own dilemma and, by extension, the dilemma of the modern artist. To use the symbolism of "The Lady of Shalott" and its retelling as "Lancelot and Elaine," the tower and the city remain in opposition to each other. The artist's expression of truth as he sees it is almost inevitably compromised by the perceptions of other men. Nevertheless, his grasp of the truth is valid and timeless. Guinevere realizes this at the last when she says, "We needs must love the highest when we see it" ("Guinevere," l. 655). The artist's truth is more real than life and at the same time beyond life in a region where the mists which shroud Camelot are dissolved into empyreal clarity. And so, if the mystical truth vouchsafed to artists is more real than earthly reality, it cannot ultimately be expressed in reality.

The awareness of this opposition does not, however, relieve the artist of the responsibility to express his vision in reality. It would undoubtedly be easier for an artist to retreat to the tower and live in solitude with his vision, to "Let visions of the night or of the day / Come as they will."

But the artist, like the King, "must guard / That which he rules . . . and may not wander from the allotted field" ("The Holy Grail," ll. 901–907). His gift comes "from the great deep"; his vision is an intimation of an ideality, of which all things physical are but fleeting manifestations allowed to the aesthetic perceptions of the artist.

The *Idylls* are the work of many years. Like Wagner's *Ring,* also written over a span of years, the *Idylls* represent the artist's efforts to find the proper vehicle to set forth what he had to say about art, morality, and the whole spiritual life of man. The idyllic form alone, Tennyson found, permitted him to make these observations without the necessity of intruding, *qua* poet, into his subject. The progression from "Mariana" of 1830 to the last published of the *Idylls of the King,* "Balin and Balan," in 1885, is the history of Tennyson's endeavor to render, by means of a viable objective form, his own inner awareness. In these "summaries of mighty dramas," as Hallam described the idylls of 1830, Tennyson blended the dramatic, narrative, and lyric to produce a new kind of poetry in English; and in the *Idylls* he solved, to a great degree, the problem of the long poem for modern literature.

II

The tableland of life

Few of Tennyson's ideas find more frequent expression in his poetry or in his biography than his belief in the illusory nature of time and space. From the early "Armageddon" through *In Memoriam* to the late "The Ancient Sage," Tennyson presents human existence as separation from Eternal Reality, as, in metaphorical terms, an uncertain land area situated between two great bodies of water. Occasionally, in our most inspired moments, he says, we have glimpses of that immortal sea from which we came and to which we are to return, but most often the spiritual deeps are hidden from us by a veil as we bide our time here on this time-locked sphere.

In one of his most important religious poems, "De Profundis," Tennyson directly employs the metaphor of the sea in speaking of man's origin. "Out of the deep" the child is said to come, "banished into mystery" from his spiritual home. In his earthly life the child is cut off from the eternal by time, "our mortal veil / And shatter'd phantom of that infinite One"; for "our world is but the bounding shore" of the "true world." In life, then, we stand veiled from "Infinite Ideality, Immeasurable Reality, Infinite Personality," and we know, consequently, only the illusion, only space and time, never the reality itself. As the speaker in "The Ancient Sage" says, man waits "watching from a phantom shore" for "The phantom walls of this illusion [to] fade." Or in the better known lines of "Crossing the Bar," "from out our bourne of Time and Place" we wait for that which came from out the boundless deep to take us home again.

In the *Idylls of the King* Tennyson makes brilliant use of the sea and associated imagery to underscore this concept and to provide a structure for the twelve idylls. "Birth is a mystery and death is a mystery," he said in commenting on the *Idylls,* "and in the midst lies the tableland of life, and its struggles and performances" (*Memoir,* II, 127). Often Tennyson's remarks on his poetry serve only to illuminate the obvious or to obfuscate the complex, but this particular comment seems to me of great value in helping us understand the poem. For it points to the relationship between time and eternity which, in my opinion, is one of the central themes of the *Idylls.*

The evanescent quality of Arthur's kingdom is suggested first of all by the multiplicity of cyclical images in the *Idylls,* which serve to emphasize that what comes into being must eventually fade and die. One of the basic structural devices of the poem is the cycle of the seasons, by which the poem proceeds from spring in the opening idyll to winter in the final one. This is of course emblematic of the fate of Arthur's kingdom as it moves from vitality and success to the blighting and death of all high hopes which nurtured its beginning.

Within this basic framework many of the individual idylls move through cycles of their own. "The Holy Grail," for example, is structured loosely around the cycle of the year, taking place within "a year and a day." "Gareth and Lynette" suggests the cycle of the day, or perhaps man's life on earth, in Gareth's encounter with the four brothers—Morning-Star, Noonday-Sun, Evening-Sun, and Night. Finally, in "The Passing of Arthur" the action takes place within a day's time, moving from dawn to dawn.

Another such device is the beast imagery. Arthur begins by wresting the land from the beasts and driving out the beast in man. As the *Idylls* progresses there is a gradual return to bestiality until the cycle is completed and Arthur cries in anguish: "and all my realm / Reels back into the beast and is no more" ("The Passing of Arthur," ll. 25–26).[1]

The third structural device suggesting the evanescent quality of Camelot is the sea imagery, which so far as I can learn has gone unnoticed. These sea images occur mainly in the first and last, or frame idylls, serving to suggest the separation of the temporal from the eternal. "The Coming of Arthur" is especially rich in images pertaining to the sea. First, there is the account of Arthur's birth: on the night of Uther's death the mages Bleys and Merlin stroll to the edge of the sea, and suddenly

1 See Edward Engelberg, "The Beast Image in Tennyson's *Idylls of the King*," *ELH*, XXII (1955), 287–292.

Descending thro' the dismal night—a night
In which the bounds of heaven and earth were lost—
Beheld, so high upon the dreary deeps
It seem'd in heaven, a ship, the shape thereof
A dragon wing'd, and all from stem to stern
Bright with a shining people on the decks,
And gone as soon as seen. And then the two
Dropt to the cove, and watch'd the great sea fall,
Wave after wave, each mightier than the last,
Till last, a ninth one, gathering half the deep
And full of voices, slowly rose and plunged
Roaring, and all the wave was in a flame;
And down the wave and in the flame was borne
A naked babe, and rode to Merlin's feet,
Who stoopt and caught the babe, and cried, "The King!
Here is an heir for Uther!" And the fringe
Of that great breaker, sweeping up the strand,
Lash'd at the wizard as he spake the word,
And all at once all round him rose in fire,
So that the child and he were clothed in fire.

(ll. 370–389)

To one familiar with the themes and images of Tennyson's earlier verse this narrative is a clear sign of the heaven-blessed nature of Arthur's birth. For the image of the ship from without the deep served most importantly in Lyric CIII of *In Memoriam,* in which the speaker finds reunion with the dead Hallam, to indicate the meeting of the temporal and eternal at a climactic moment of the poem. In the lyric "Tears, Idle Tears," to cite but one other example, the image of the ship is used much to the same effect. The point which Tennyson wishes to make, and which he is unwilling for us to overlook, is that Arthur comes to earth from the spiritual deep and that his coming serves to mediate between time and eternity. The instant of his coming was one of those timeless moments which Tennyson speaks of throughout his poetry: it was, we are told, a night "In which the bounds of heaven and earth were lost."

In this first idyll all that Arthur does has the blessing of the deep. At the formation of the Round Table appears the Lady of the Lake, who is said to dwell

> *Down in a deep—calm, whatsoever storms*
> *May shake the world—and when the surface rolls,*
> *Hath power to walk the waters like our Lord.*

(ll. 291–293)

The Lady gives Arthur the mystic sword and blesses the confraternity by sending forth "A voice as of the waters" (l. 290). Likewise, at the wedding of Arthur and Guinevere there comes "A voice as of the waters" (l. 464) blessing their union.

Merlin's song in riddling triplets suggests the use of cyclical imagery in the *Idylls:*

> *Rain, sun and rain! and the free blossom blows;*
> *Sun, rain, and sun! and where is he who knows?*
> *From the great deep to the great deep he goes.*

(ll. 408–410)

The sun-rain cycle, employed in the later idylls, is the cycle of nature, the life-giving cycle producing flowers and grain, while the refrain "From the great deep to the great deep he goes" suggests the cycle of life from eternity to eternity.

Also here in the first idyll we are introduced to another

water image which will play such a large part in the closing idylls. As the narrative grows further away from Arthur's coming from the sea we gradually see settling over the action of the poem a haze and mist. The Lady of the Lake appears enshrouded in mist: "A mist / Of incense curl'd about her, and her face / Wellnigh was hidden in the minster gloom" (ll. 286–288). Leodogran's dream, occurring at the moment when he is debating whether to give his daughter Guinevere to Arthur, is of a "phantom king" surrounded by haze. Suddenly the dream changes: "the haze / Descended, and the solid earth became / As nothing, but the King stood out in heaven, / Crown'd" (ll. 440–443). And so with the closing of the first idyll we are prepared to see action in a moment of time arrested from the round of eternity, a moment when the hero with the authority of the spiritual deep comes to change the old order.

With the beginning of the ten idylls grouped under the heading "The Round Table" we are presented with another water image, this time flowing water. The opening lines of "Gareth and Lynette" are concerned with this very image:

> The last tall son of Lot and Bellicent,
> And tallest, Gareth, in a showerful spring
> Stared at the spate. A slender-shafted pine
> Lost footing, fell, and so was whirl'd away.
> "How he went down," said Gareth, "as a false knight
> Or evil king before my lance, if lance
> Were mine to use—O senseless cataract,
> Bearing all down in thy precipitancy—
> And yet thou art but swollen with cold snows
> And mine is living blood.

(ll. 1–10)

This passage about the rushing stream is pertinent to the main action of the idyll: the pine which is carried away by the flood is contrasted with Gareth's own feeling of domestic imprisonment away from Camelot. The purpose of this imagery is, I believe, not only to indicate the flowing of the action of the poem away from the waters of the great deep but also to represent the flux of time or experience in time. The use of flowing water in this sense is not uncommon in Tennyson: we find it, for example, in the early poem "The Mystic," where the entranced spirit is said to hear "Time flowing in the middle of the night, / And all things creeping to a day of doom."

Flowing water is used perhaps to best effect in "Lancelot and Elaine." The Lily Maid dwells beside the river in childhood, never partaking of what is symbolically the stream of life. She lives "in fantasy," caught up in her dream of reality and seeing life only as she preconceives it. It is only after her venture into the world of experience, as represented by her encounter with Lancelot, that she journeys on the river. Ironically, her river voyage, representing, I suppose, a journey into the reality of the city of Camelot from her life in the tower, becomes symbolic not only of the life she has missed but also of her journey into timelessness. The device of the river journey we find often in Tennyson. Indeed, it is central to such early poems as "Recollections of the Arabian Nights" and "The Lady of Shalott," which of course is an earlier version of the Elaine idyll.

The voyage is also used to somewhat the same ironic effect in "Merlin and Vivien." Mainly as a result of his encounter with Vivien, who with her malicious slander is said to leave "Death in the living waters" of Camelot (l. 146), Merlin journeys in a boat to Brittany to escape the melancholy which had fallen on him in Camelot. But as it turns out, Merlin is accompanied on this voyage by the very thing which he had hoped to elude—namely, Vivien. And this evil encountered in the isolation of the woods of Broceliande is far more overwhelming than it ever was at Camelot. Thus the water journey which supposedly was to be regenerative for the mage becomes a journey into death. Furthermore, the rainstorm at the close of the idyll does not refresh the old man and help him to triumph over the insidious evil which Vivien represents, as first it seemed it was to do; on the contrary, the rain drives Merlin to accept Vivien into his embrace and consequently leads to his ruin.

In "The Holy Grail" water imagery is used to the same ambiguous effect. The Cup itself appears to the knights during a storm. As I shall attempt to show in my chapter on this idyll, the Grail becomes a symbol not only of regeneration but also of destruction, and the fact that the Grail is associated with water helps to reinforce the dual meaning of the water imagery. The water journey takes on perhaps its most complex meaning in the account of Lancelot's quest after the Grail. After a series of adventures in a wasteland, he at last finds a boat at a water's edge. "I will embark and I will lose myself," he says to himself in his madness (l. 802). He lands and finally has a clouded vision of the Holy Grail, but he is not certain of the validity of the vision. Here, it seems to me, Tennyson has with great skill used the theme of the water journey: it becomes symbolic of the voyage of the imagination into a visionary realm and, within context, also emblematic of a kind of death in time. For Lancelot sees and does not see: he is given new life as a result of the experience but he also denies himself the possession of this new life when he refuses to disentangle himself from Guinevere. As it ends up, however, he does finally act on his vision when, we are later told, he gives himself over to the religious life.

In "The Last Tournament" the water journey is used to indicate restlessness and indecision in time. Tristram travels back and forth between Tintagil and Brittany, unable to possess fully the Isolt whom he loves, or thinks he loves, and, on the other hand, unable to love the Isolt he possesses. Tristram is never able to find the proper channel for his energies: in reaction to the King's idealism, which he sees is incapable of perfecting mankind, he turns, at one instant, to the illicit affair with the British Isolt and, at the next, to the domestic life with the Isolt of Brittany. Unsatisfied, however, he returns over the sea to renew his sensual love with Mark's wife. Tristram, we see—and I do not think it fanciful to find in his journeyings over the sea a representation of his aimlessness—is literally adrift on the sea of life.

Also in "The Last Tournament" we find in Tristram's song the use of a water image which apparently refers to Arthur. In his song of the two stars Tristram sings: "And one was water and one star was fire, / And one will ever shine and one will pass" (ll. 730–731). Clearly if this lyric has any relevance at all to the meaning of the poem, we must understand the water as Arthur, or Arthur's ideals, and the fire as illicit passion.

Throughout "The Round Table" the haze and mist which enveloped the last lines of "The Coming of Arthur" recur only when there is allusion to those beings or entities which originate in the spiritual deep. "Gareth and Lynette," the first of the ten idylls comprising "The Round Table," opens with a spring shower and proceeds to brilliant sunlight. The mist of the beginning frame idyll manifests itself here only when Gareth sees Camelot in the distance. Arthur's kingdom first appears to Gareth and his companions enshrouded in mist, although at times the spires prick through:

> Far off they saw the silver-misty morn
> Rolling her smoke about the royal mount,
> That rose between the forest and the field.
> At times the summit of the high city flash'd;
> At times the spires and turrets half-way down
> Prick'd thro' the mist; at times the great gate shone
> Only, that open'd on the field below;
> Anon, the whole fair city had disappear'd.
>
> (ll. 186–193)

The mist so obscures and seemingly enchants the city that Gareth doubts its reality. He tells Merlin:

> Your city moved so weirdly in the mist—
> Doubt if the King be king at all, or come
> From Fairyland; and whether this be built
> By magic, and by fairy kings and queens;
> Or whether there be any city at all,
> Or all a vision.
>
> (ll. 241–246)

Merlin's apocalyptic dream of the end of Arthur's kingdom is of "An ever-moaning battle in the mist" ("Merlin
and Vivien," l. 190). When as a boy Arthur finds a crown of
diamonds in a misty glen and places it on his head, a voice
from out the "misty moonshine" tells him that he shall be
king ("Lancelot and Elaine," ll. 35–55). The Holy Grail
appears unto the knights veiled in a "luminous cloud," a
figure suggesting not only the possible unreality of the Cup
but also its function as mediator between time and eternity.

The use of mist as the barrier between time and eternity
is employed tellingly in "Merlin and Vivien." As a result of
his dream of the destruction of Camelot, Merlin finds himself caught up in a gloomy mist. He thinks of himself as
lying on a shore watching a huge wave about to break, a
wave which will "sweep me from my hold upon the world, /
My use and name and fame" (ll. 301–302). Furthermore, he
tells Vivien, when he looks upon the "single misty star" in
the sword of Orion which is surrounded by the great nebula,
he fancies "some vast charm concluded in that star / To
make fame nothing" (ll. 506–511). Eventually, of course, the
great wave, ironically in the person of Vivien, does break
upon him and he is lost to the "life and use and name and
fame" of the land world.

By the time we reach the last idyll of "The Round Table"
the mist has so veiled the setting that we can hardly see the
action. "Guinevere" opens upon a motionless landscape
barely visible: "The white mist, like a face-cloth to the face, /
Clung to the dead earth, and the land was still." Arthur himself has now also become enveloped in the mist: so little is

he now king, so little a human figure acting authoritatively, that he seems partially swallowed up by the great deep which impinges upon the land to claim him. Thus Guinevere's last sight of her husband is of a form enshrouded in the mist—Arthur, we are told, "seem'd the phantom of a giant in it"; finally, "himself became as mist / Before her, moving ghostlike to his doom." We are reminded here of Leodogran's dream in which the authority of Arthur's kingship is vouchsafed to Guinevere's father; for what Guinevere finally sees—and unfortunately it is not until the end that she sees—is what her father saw in the beginning: a phantasmal figure transcending the mists which bar passage from the world of time to the realm of eternity. She does not see his face, which, the narrator tells us, "then was as an angel's," but she sees "Wet with the mists and smitten by the lights, / The Dragon of the great Pendragonship / Blaze, making all the night a steam of fire" (ll. 591–601).

In the final idyll we are shown the passing of Arthur. The idyll is, I think I should point out even at the expense of being obvious, appropriately named, because what we witness is not the *death* of the King but, rather, his *passing* from one world to another. On the day of the last battle "A death-white mist slept over sand and sea" (l. 95). This is an important detail: here the time-locked land and the timeless sea begin to blend into one another through the agency of the mist. Within the mist takes place the battle, which is described as a horrifying *danse macabre*. Finally, the battle over, the mist is blown away: "A bitter wind . . . blew / This mist aside, and with that wind the tide / Rose" (ll. 124–

126). The King stands fully revealed, as in Leodogran's dream, when he nears reunion with the deep. The sea now begins its steady encroachment upon the land, just as on the night of Arthur's birth:

> *no man was moving there;*
> *Nor any cry of Christian heard thereon,*
> *Nor yet of heathen; only the wan wave*
> *Brake in among dead faces, to and fro*
> *Swaying the helpless hands, and up and down*
> *Tumbling the hollow helmets of the fallen,*
> *And shiver'd brands that once had fought with Rome.*
> *And rolling far along the gloomy shores*
> *The voice of days of old and days to be.*
>
> (ll. 127–135)

"Hearest thou this great voice that shakes the world," the King asks Bedivere,

> *And wastes the narrow realm whereon we move,*
> *And beats upon the faces of the dead,*
> *My dead, as tho' they had not died for me?*
>
> (ll. 139–141)

Here we find Arthur himself identifying the sea with eternity, thus heightening the significance of the sea's intrusion upon his "narrow realm." His work done, the time is now at hand for Arthur to be redeemed from time and for Excalibur, the gift from the deep and sign of Arthur's active power, to be returned to the Lady of the Lake.

The geographical details in the closing lines are important because they serve to symbolize the relationship between time and eternity which Tennyson had been at such pains to establish in the preceding idylls. Bedivere bears

Arthur to a spot which "stood on a dark strait of barren land. / On one side lay the Ocean, and on one / Lay a great water" (ll. 178–180). Here we find symbolized Arthur's situation: he comes from the sea to stand for a while on the strands of time and, finally, to pass on to another body of water leading to the sea; in other words, we perceive that Arthur's kingdom exists in a moment of time arrested from the round of eternity.

Like Tennyson's earlier creation Ulysses, Arthur hears the deep moan round with many voices as he goes to the shore, where he is to meet the barge which will bear him away, as it did the young Elaine, to another world—"Down that long water opening on the deep" (l. 466). As Arthur is carried off, Bedivere recalls Merlin's "weird rhyme": "From the great deep to the great deep he goes" (l. 445). The cycle has been completed: Arthur is transported back into timelessness and the sea of eternity literally and figuratively flows over his temporal kingdom.

We learn from the *Idylls of the King,* therefore, that for Tennyson space and time constitute the *principium individuationis* which divides life into distinct organisms in different places and periods. Man's existence in the world of time is life among land shadows where he is cut off, as the poet wrote in "De Profundis," from the "true world" of the deep. Man and his world, accordingly, are only phenomenal. In reality there is only the "whole World-self and all in all." Indeed, to quote again Tennyson's own comment on his poem, "Birth is a mystery and death is a mystery and in the midst lies the tableland of life."

III

The moral paradox of the hero

For Tennyson, as for other modern thinkers, the starting point of all philosophy lies in the reality of self. As C. F. G. Masterman, in his much neglected book on Tennyson's religious thought, has shown, the self for Tennyson "is the one and only thing of which by direct conviction we can assert reality." [1] Yet, the question remains, how is the self to be apprehended? This problem of identity is, I believe, central in Tennyson's poetry, and indeed it may justly be said that the great body of his poetry is directed toward answering the question. In this chapter I should like to suggest, by first briefly examining some of Tennyson's earlier verse, that the problem of self and its relation to objects in terms of moral experience is vital to an understanding of the *Idylls of the King*.

According to Tennyson, the child has no sense of identity, "Has never thought that 'this is I' "; but gradually he learns that he is distinct from other forms of life, "learns the use of

---

[1] C. F. G. Masterman, *Tennyson as a Religious Teacher* (Boston, 1900), p. 61.

'I' and 'Me,' " and with this knowledge of "a separate mind" "His isolation grows defined" (*In Memoriam,* XLV). Thus through cognition the self is first apprehended. But this awareness of self is only partial, since the self in isolation cannot know its relationship to the objects outside self which constitute the phenomenal world. Tennyson insists that one never knows himself through introspection, a position maintained, for example, in "The Palace of Art." The problem then is to bring the world which seems to be independent of the self into the experience of the self. But how is this to be effected?

In "The Lady of Shalott" Tennyson traces allegorically the means by which the question may be answered. "The new-born love for something, for some one in the wide world from which she has been so long secluded," Tennyson said in reference to the poem, "takes her out of the region of shadows into that of realities" (*Memoir,* I, 117). Through love, then, the self awakens to consciousness of its own personality by bringing the not-self into its experience. The identifying power of love becomes a constant theme in Tennyson's early poetry: it is specifically the subject of *The Princess,* in which the Prince is saved from his "weird seizures" by the love of Princess Ida; of *In Memoriam,* wherein the "I" is redeemed from despair through love for his dead friend; and of "Maud," in which the hero is saved from psychic disintegration through his love for the "glorified" Maud.[2]

2 See my essays "The 'Weird Seizures' in *The Princess," Texas Studies in Literature and Language,* IV (1962), 268–275; "The 'Heav-

The problem of identity had not, however, been fully explored. There was still another way in which the self must be apprehended and which Tennyson had not carefully examined. This was the power of will, which is also an essential part of the self. Reading in German metaphysics had evidently reinforced Tennyson's conception that the not-self world of external objects exists only to the extent that one organizes it for one's actions, that things take on meaning in proportion as one uses them as means. According to this view, only when the individual has built up the world as a field of action does he realize himself as the individual who carried out that action. One thus attains knowledge of self by attacking, overcoming, and assimilating the not-self. This, of course, involves the concept of the self as willing, as choosing and imposing means; this is the part of man which is the moral agent.

In his early poetry Tennyson had treated peripherally the problem of will. In his feminine portraits he had been concerned with two types of female: the willful *femme fatale* and the violated suffering maiden whose will had been subdued.[3] "A Dream of Fair Women," for example, consciously contrasts these two types of female: Helen and Cleopatra, who bent the wills of men, and Iphigenia and Jephtha's daughter, who submitted to masculine wills. Only with *In*

enly Friend': The 'New Mythus' of *In Memoriam*," *The Personalist*, XLIII (1962), 383–402; and "Tennyson's *Maud*," *Connotation*, I (1962), 12–32; also my book *Theme and Symbol in Tennyson's Poems to 1850* (Philadelphia, 1964).

3 See Lionel Stevenson, "The 'High-Born Maiden' Symbol in Tennyson," *PMLA*, LXIII (1948), 234–244, and my essay "The 'Fatal Woman' Symbol in Tennyson," *PMLA*, LXXIV (1959), 438–443.

Memoriam, however, did Tennyson begin to undertake a philosophical consideration of volition.

In his elegy Tennyson demonstrates how in the act of volition the self strives to realize itself in the external world. In denying a mechanical conception of the universe, he enunciates that not through a deterministic scheme but through a direct certitude of our power of choice do we prove ourselves. "Free will and its relation to the meaning of human life and to circumstance," Hallam Tennyson reports of his father, "was latterly one of his most common subjects of conversation . . . 'Take away the sense of individual responsibility and men sink into pessimism and madness' " *(Memoir,* I, 316–317).

In Memoriam is not, however, primarily about realization of self through the power of will. To be sure, the poet does speak of the "living Will that shalt endure" (CXXXI) and of the fact that "Our wills are ours" (Prologue), but he does not attempt to explain how the power of choice is exemplified in man's life. Rather, *In Memoriam,* in common with Tennyson's earlier verse, treats essentially the reality of self as it is affirmed through love—through love of the dead Hallam who is enshrined as an ideal type of humanity.

As an ideal man Hallam, who is closely identified with Christ, becomes the heroic redeemer, "the noble type," who, through furthering moral development, will save mankind from extinction. "Appearing ere the times were ripe" (Epilogue), Hallam is that "herald of a higher race" (CXVIII) who will lead mankind to a perfect state of existence.

When he had completed the poem, Tennyson found that

it was far more optimistic about the fate of the human race than he himself was. "It's too hopeful, this poem, more than I am myself," he told James Knowles. "I think of adding another to it, a speculative one, bringing out the thought of the 'Higher Pantheism,' and showing that all the arguments are about as good on one side as the other, and thus throw man back more on the primitive impulses and feelings." [4]

It is partly to this concern that he devoted the *Idylls of the King*. Let us see, Tennyson seems to have said, let us see what would happen if another Arthur, "the flower of kings," were to set about redeeming the world. Would he succeed, would he be able to rid man of the beast in his nature? The answer which the completed *Idylls* gives is a pessimistic no. For here Tennyson takes up the paradox of reality—namely, how can the redeemer work his will without violating the will of others? The hero fails, Tennyson shows, not because he does not have access to value—Arthur comes from the spiritual deep—but because the value-laden will, encountering the impregnable amorality of nature, can only destroy the very values of love and freedom which it has created.

I have previously mentioned how in Tennyson's philosophy of the self things take on meaning in proportion as one uses them as means and how the objects of the world become implements. At this point I should also mention that to Tennyson there is a greater, an Absolute Self, of which our selves are but finite expressions; for, according to Tennyson,

---

[4] James Knowles, "A Personal Reminiscence of Tennyson," *Nineteenth Century*, XXXIII (1893), 182.

the self cannot posit itself as a finite self without simultaneously positing an infinite self. It is this experience of realizing one's self as a finite self that involves the assurance of
the self in the Absolute.

In "De Profundis" Tennyson speaks of the finite self as
part of an infinite creative power and how as such the finite
self is always engaged in the process of creation. For Tennyson this creation is moral, the choosing between "the grain
and husk," since by the very act of choice man builds up the
world for himself in terms of his duties. The "main miracle,"
he addresses his infant son, is "that thou art thou, / With
power on thine act and on the world." Hallam Tennyson
tells us that his father "held that there was an intimate con-
nexion between the human and the divine, and that each individual will had a spiritual and eternal significance with
relation to other individual wills as well as to the Supreme
and Eternal Will" (*Memoir*, I, 319). The greater the task
the individual undertakes, the larger, more effective self he
becomes. Thus the great man assimilates as many objects
and individuals as he possibly can, taking them over into
himself. This assimilation, however, presents its own moral
problem; for in attacking and overcoming the not-self, man
violates the freedom of those individuals assimilated into his
experience. It is this moral paradox that Tennyson turns his
attention to in the *Idylls of the King*.

Arthur appears as "Ideal manhood closed in real man"
and the "stainless gentleman." He comes from the realm of
pure value to impart these values to the world, to rid the
land of beast and pagan and to establish an ideal kingdom

on earth. But at first his authority is not generally recognized: men debate whether he is really the rightful heir to the throne:

> *No king of ours! a son of Gorloïs he,*
> *Or else the child of Anton, and no king,*
> *Or else baseborn.*
>
> ("The Coming of Arthur," ll. 231–233)

Arthur must, therefore, impose his authority by force: in battle he subdues his enemies; but more insidiously, he binds his knights to his will with "so straight vows to himself" that they are as "dazed, as one who wakes / Half-blinded at the coming of a light" ("The Coming of Arthur," ll. 261–265). In accepting his will they deny their own; in attempting to take on the personality of the King they annihilate their own personalities. During the early days of the Round Table, Bellicent relates, when Arthur spoke,

> *I beheld*
> *From eye to eye thro' all their Order flash*
> *A momentary likeness of the King.*
>
> ("The Coming of Arthur," ll. 268–270)

As a kind of New Jerusalem Arthur has Merlin, the great artificer, build the glorious city of Camelot, which did "spire to heaven" ("Gareth and Lynette," ll. 296–302). This is, says Merlin, a city built to music, symbol of the harmony obtaining between Arthur and his knights when their wills are one. Camelot is, therefore, the objective embodiment of Arthur's will, a city always in the process of creation, "seeing the city is built / To music, therefore never built at all"

("Gareth and Lynette," ll. 272–273).[5] Merlin alone, however, understands this phenomenon; indeed, he alone foresees the outcome of Arthur's undertaking. "A young man will be wiser by and by," he says in his riddling triplets ("The Coming of Arthur," l. 403), apparently meaning that Arthur will eventually learn that he cannot make the world the ideal realm which he envisions. Merlin knows, even so early as "Gareth and Lynette," that disintegration of personality has already set in among the inhabitants of Arthur's city: "For there is nothing in it as it seems / Saving the King" (ll. 206–261). By imposing his will on the inhabitants of Camelot, Arthur has caused his people to accept the delusion that they are other than they are. Go not into the city, Merlin tells Gareth, for if you do you will become

> *A thrall to his enchantments, for the King*
> *Will bind thee by such vows as is a shame*
> *A man should not be bound by, yet the which*
> *No man can keep.*

(ll. 265–268)

By enjoining upon his knights these impossible vows Arthur creates the condition which causes guilt and madness throughout his Order. As Tennyson said, "Take away the sense of individual responsibility and men sink into pessimism and madness." "My knights," says Arthur,

---

[5] It is interesting to note that Schopenhauer, in *The World as Will and Idea*, Bk. III, defined music as *"the copy of the will itself, whose objectivity the Ideas are"* (*The Philosophy of Schopenhauer*, ed. Irwin Edman [New York, 1928,] p. 201).

> *are sworn to vows*
> *Of utter hardihood, utter gentleness,*
> *And, loving, utter faithfulness in love,*
> *And uttermost obedience to the King.*
>
> ("Gareth and Lynette," ll. 541–544)

In other words, Arthur would have his followers become ideals.

The traditional interpretation of the *Idylls* is that Arthur's kingdom falls because of the adulterous relationship between Lancelot and Guinevere. Against such an interpretation I would argue that decay has already set in before there is any mention of their guilt. Sir Kay is as boorish as, perhaps more so than, any of the antagonists to Arthur's cause. He fails in gentleness, courtesy, and obedience to the King; he is but the first we meet who does not live up to his vows. For we see as the *Idylls* progresses that by volitional violation Arthur creates the necessity for emotional dependency: being not themselves but pale facsimiles of the King, his knights must depend more and more on someone or something for emotional satisfaction.

Lancelot's and Guinevere's sin is thus, I believe, not the cause but the symptom of what is wrong in Camelot. Arthur has attempted to take Guinevere completely unto himself, to refashion her according to his conceptions, to make her will his, to set her up as the feminine ideal; and he forces this view of her—that is, Guinevere as the feminine counterpart to the ideal man—on his Order. Guinevere is not, however, made of the same metal as the King. A real woman and not an abstract ideal presence, she has all the passion and longing for life of a normal woman. In this world of illusions where, says Merlin, all is "Confusion, and illusion, and relation, / Elusion, and occasion, and evasion" ("Gareth and Lynette," ll. 281–282), Guinevere suffers the same delusions as everybody else. This is made manifestly the case when in "The Coming of Arthur" Guinevere mistakes Lancelot for the King. It is not surprising, therefore, that even the rumor of an illicit sexual relationship on the part of the Queen is enough to disenchant the knights of the Round Table. They have been forced to believe in an ideal; and when they see that their ideal is merely human after all and subject to the same delusions and faults as real people, they immediately are led to suspect that nothing is true—neither the idea of the Round Table nor their loved ones.

This is first brought out in "The Marriage of Geraint," wherein Geraint is led to suspect Enid of unfaithfulness because of the rumor concerning the unfaithfulness of the Queen. In one of the few passages in the *Idylls* in which the author speaks in his own voice, Tennyson says that we as men "forge a lifelong trouble for ourselves, / By taking true for false, or false for true" ("Geraint and Enid," ll. 3–4).

The theme of emotional dependency is strikingly brought out in "Balin and Balan." Because Arthur has demanded so much of his knights, Balin feels that he can never hope to attain the refinement, the gentleness and courtesy required of the Round Table: "These be gifts," wails Balin, "Born with the blood, not learnable, divine, / Beyond *my* reach" (ll. 170–172). Feeling strongly a sense of inadequacy, Balin has to have an emotional prop in order to remain sane. He is, like the other knights of the Round Table, except perhaps Gareth, morbidly dependent on others. Balan is at first his means of balance, and when Balan leaves he is emotionally lost. He looks around and sees Lancelot as the likeliest ideal to imitate, but he despairs of ever achieving the perfection of courtesy that is Lancelot's. Moreover, he perceives that Lancelot is emotionally dependent on the Queen. So Balin likewise turns to Guinevere: "Her likewise would I worship an I might" (l. 180). He requests her emblem for his shield, and the crown royal is granted him. This symbol of the Queen becomes his emotional prop:

> *So Balin bare the crown, and all the knights*
> *Approved him, and the Queen; and all the world*
> *Made music, and he felt his being move*
> *In music with his Order and the King.*
>
> (ll. 205–208)

Supported by this prop he is able to go on. When he sees Guinevere and Lancelot in the garden, he undergoes a catastrophic shock: his prop begins to fail him and in distress he runs to the woods, away from Arthur's civilization.

By the time he reaches Pellam's castle, however, Balin has completely suppressed his doubts about the Queen. When Garlon insults his emotional prop, he is outraged, mainly because he himself is insecure on this point, and kills Garlon on the spot. For the murder he feels guilty and unworthy of the quite unrealistic idea he has of the Queen. He therefore hangs his shield on a tree, determined to carry it no more. Significantly though, he does not ride off and leave the shield behind; instead, he casts himself on the ground under it and mopes. He cannot leave the shield because even though he feels unworthy of it, he has to have a prop of some sort. To leave it behind would make him defenseless not only physically but emotionally as well. Furthermore, he cannot return to Camelot for fear of what he might discover about the Queen. He has already learned too much for his own comfort and has suppressed what he has found out; any more discoveries would be fatal. This is why his reaction to Vivien, who tells him what he most feared of finding out, is so violent. Balin, consequently, goes out of his mind. Turning against the thing on which he is most dependent, he stamps the shield to ruin.

In the idylls immediately following "Balin and Balan" reference is frequently made to the impossible constraints which Arthur has placed on his knights. Merlin laments:

> *O selfless man and stainless gentleman,*
> *Who wouldst against thine own eye-witness fain*
> *Have all men true and leal, all women pure!*
>
> ("Merlin and Vivien," ll. 790–792)

And Guinevere speaks of Arthur as the unsatisfactory husband because he is so

> *Rapt in this fancy of his Table Round,*
> *And swearing men to vows impossible,*
> *To make them like himself.*
>
> ("Lancelot and Elaine," ll. 129–131)

Guinevere is, after Merlin, the first to see the fault in Arthur; she perceives that it is the King's very fault to be faultless and to wish the world like himself. Arthur, she sees,

is a monomaniac, a blameless man who seeks to eradicate all
blame from the world, a heroic redeemer who would impose
his values on the universe. "No keener hunter after glory
breathes," the Queen tells Lancelot. "He loves it in his
knights more than himself; / They prove to him his work"
("Lancelot and Elaine," ll. 155–157). In other words, Arthur
realizes himself by seeing his values projected onto his
knights. The men of the Round Table become, therefore,
objects as means, not objects as ends; they are valuable in
that they provide the proving ground of the values of the
King.

The knights having been emotionally exploited, the way
is prepared for the outstanding example of emotional dependency in the *Idylls*—namely, the Grail quest in "The
Holy Grail." As I pointed out in the case of Balin, the characters in the *Idylls,* their sense of identity having been
violated, are dependent on some kind of prop for emotional
stability. This is provided in this idyll by the vision of the
Holy Grail, which becomes a kind of compensation for each
of the knights who goes on the quest. Lancelot seeks the
Grail as a compensation for his dependency on Guinevere;
he attempts, in other words, to replace one prop with another. Yet when he is deprived of the presence of Guinevere
he completely loses all sense of identity:

> *And forth I went, and while I yearn'd and strove*
> *To tear the twain [the wholesome and the poisonous] asunder*
>   *in my heart,*
> *My madness came upon me as of old. . . .*
>
> (ll. 782–784)

Bors, totally dependent on his cousin Lancelot, apparently quests for the Grail because Lancelot does so; in fact, he would have gladly foregone his vision of the Cup:

> *He well had been content*
> *Not to have seen, so Lancelot might have seen*
> *The Holy Cup of healing.*

(ll. 650–652)

Percivale undertakes the quest presumably because he is dissatisfied with the life of Camelot; he was tired of

> *all vainglories, rivalries,*
> *And earthly heats that spring and sparkle out*
> *Among us in the jousts, while women watch*
> *Who wins, who falls, and waste the spiritual strength*
> *Within us, better offer'd up to heaven.*

(ll. 32–36)

Indeed, the alacrity with which the knights jump at the chance to go on the Grail quest suggests the hollowness of their lives and their dissatisfaction with the life they are leading. But Percivale's dependency on Camelot and on Arthur is evidenced by the fact that in his isolation on the quest he, like the others, goes to pieces; his sense of personal identity must be confirmed by others. As soon as he leaves Camelot he enters into a sort of surrealistic hell of the imagination, and it is only through the instrumentation of Galahad that he is allowed to see the Grail even in the distance. Gawain's motivation for undertaking the quest is simply that the other knights do so.

The most interesting case of the Grail knights is Gala-

had's. He goes on the quest because he has lost himself by
sitting in the Siege Perilous and taken on the identity of the
nun, Percivale's sister. In his semi-dramatic monologue,
Percivale, without any clear understanding of what he is
relating, informs us of this fact. When Galahad first heard
of the nun's vision, "His eyes became so like her own," Percivale reports, "they seem'd / Hers, and himself her brother
more than I" (ll. 141–142). The nun makes a sword-belt of
her hair and binds this on Galahad, saying:

> *My knight, my love, my knight of heaven,*
> *O thou, my love, whose love is one with mine,*
> *I, maiden, round thee, maiden, bind my belt.*
> *Go forth, for thou shalt see what I have seen. . . .*

And, Percivale relates,

> *as she spake*
> *She sent the deathless passion in her eyes*
> *Thro' him, and made him hers, and laid her mind*
> *On him, and he believed in her belief.*
>
> (ll. 157–165)

The Grail quest seems to stem, then, from emotional frustration, resulting in the loss of identity, and from the desire
to find a support to stabilize a new identity. Ultimately the
quest is a manifestation of the knights' attempt to exchange
the vows to the King for the vows to a vision. This is, of
course, a form of escapism, as is Balin's mad flight away from
Camelot. Guinevere is right when she shrieks, "This madness has come on us for our sins" (l. 157); and Gawain too
is right when he says to Percivale, "Thy holy nun and thou

have driven men mad, / Yea, made our mightiest madder than our least" (ll. 859–860). As Tennyson said, I repeat, "Take away the sense of individual responsibility and men sink into pessimism and madness."

The loss to Arthur resulting from the Grail quest is symbolized by the semi-destruction of Camelot which the knights find upon their return. The city built to music, the objective embodiment of Arthur's will, is no longer of one piece: the harmony of his will and that of his Order has now become cacophony. The vows to the Grail, to something other than himself, have taken precedence over the vows to the King, and dissonance is becoming more and more the dominant pattern. The loss to Arthur's identity is indicated by the partial destruction of the statue of the King which had been fashioned by Merlin.

In "Pelleas and Ettarre" we have another example of madness resulting from the ideals forced on his knights by Arthur. Pelleas surrenders his will first to Arthur and then to Ettarre, becoming totally dependent on the lady. When he finds her false, and, worse, Gawain false also, he completely foreswears the high ideals enjoined upon him. The King, he wails, "Hath made us fools and liars. O noble vows!" (l. 470); and to the hall of Arthur he groans, "Black nest of rats . . . , ye build too high" (l. 544).

At the end of "Pelleas and Ettarre" Modred says, "The time is hard at hand"; and indeed the time for the dissolution of Arthur's ideals has come. For in "The Last Tournament" we see that the Order no longer moves to music, no longer harmonizes with the King's will. The Red Knight,

who is undoubtedly Pelleas, establishes a kingdom in the
north which is founded on principles exactly the opposite of
Arthur's: the members of this northern Round Table have
no ideals imposed upon them and "profess / To be none
other than themselves" (ll. 82–83). Tristram, little Dagonet
says, has broken the King's music, and, Dagonet implies, the
fault is at least partly the King's. Arthur is "the king of
fools" because he

> *Conceits himself as God that he can make*
> *Figs out of thistles, silk from bristles, milk*
> *From burning spurge, honey from hornet-combs,*
> *And men from beasts.*
>
> (ll. 354–358)

Here we are reminded of Merlin's words that Arthur's vows
are impossible to keep but that it is a shame a man should
not be able to do so. In half praise and dispraise Dagonet
cries, "Long live the king of fools."

"The Last Tournament" ends with a long passage devoted to Tristram's consideration of the vows which the
King has imposed upon him. "The vow that binds too
strictly snaps itself," he says; and "being snapt— / We run
more counter to the soul thereof / Than had we never
sworn" (ll. 652–655). Further he says:

> *The vows!*
> *O ay—the wholesome madness of an hour—*
> *They served their use, their time; for every knight*
> *Believed himself a greater than himself,*
> *And every follower eyed him as a God;*
> *Till he, being lifted up beyond himself,*

Did mightier deeds than elsewhere he had done,
And so the realm was made. But then their vows—
First mainly thro' that sullying of our Queen—
Began to gall the knighthood, asking whence
Had Arthur right to bind them to himself?
Dropt down from heaven? wash'd up from out the deep?
They fail'd to trace him thro' the flesh and blood
Of our old kings. Whence then? a doubtful lord
To bind them by inviolable vows,
Which flesh and blood perforce would violate;
For feel this arm of mine—the tide within
Red with free chase and heather-scented air,
Pulsing full man. Can Arthur make me pure
As any maiden child? lock up my tongue
From uttering freely what I freely hear?
Bind me to one? The wide world laughs at it.
And worldling of the world am I, and know
The ptarmigan that whitens ere his hour
Woos his own end; we are not angels here
Nor shall be.

(ll. 669–694)

All this may sound like pure rationalization, Tristram's ex-
cuse for having broken the vows of purity. But we are struck
by the appositeness of his analysis when we remember that
Guinevere and Pelleas, *inter alia,* had made the same analysis. Moreover, we see that the violation of Tristram's will
has made him entirely dependent on Isolt: as the shield is
to Balin and the Holy Cup to the Grail knights, so Isolt is
to Tristram.

"Guinevere" is, I think, in part a defense of the Queen.
In a trancelike reminiscence she recalls how she had first
felt about the King after Lancelot had brought her to
Camelot: she "thought him cold, / High, self-contain'd, and

passionless, not like him, / 'Not like my Lancelot' " (ll. 402–
404). And then the King enters. Critics have objected that
Arthur here speaks like a prig, and so indeed he does. For
Arthur is the redeemer, the hero from the realm of pure
value who is more messiah than man; he is exactly what
Tennyson said he is: an ideal man—and the ideal man simply does not talk like the usual cuckolded spouse. Arthur is,
in fact, less the wronged husband than the wronged ideal
ruler. He berates Guinevere not for having broken up a
happy home but for frustrating his ideals: "For thou hast
spoilt the purpose of my life" (l. 450). Here we are finally
forced to realize that Guinevere has all along been but a
means and not an end to Arthur. Without her he would
have been unable to

> *will my will nor work my work*
> *Wholly, nor make myself in mine own realm*
> *Victor and lord.*
>
> ("The Coming of Arthur," ll. 87–89)

He had taken Guinevere as wife in order to serve as example.
Arthur had forced his knights

> *To reverence the King, as if he were*
> *Their conscience, and their conscience as their King;*

and he had enjoined them

> *To love one maiden only, cleave to her,*
> *And worship her by years of noble deeds,*
> *Until they won her: for indeed I knew*
> *Of no more subtle master under heaven*

Than is the maiden passion for a maid,
Not only to keep down the base in man,
But teach high thought, and amiable words
And courtliness, and the desire of fame,
And love of truth, and all that makes a man.

(ll. 465–466, 472–480)

His marriage thus was to serve as a model, and its failure gave license for sin in others. Arthur has, therefore, failed to attain all his heart desired: "And all through thee!" he exclaims to Guinevere.

But Arthur is the ideal man—not the ideal husband—and so out of his "vast pity" he forgives the Queen:

Lo, I forgive thee, as Eternal God
Forgives!

(ll. 541–552)

It has frequently been pointed out that no man has the right or power to forgive as God forgives. Arthur is not, though, as I have mentioned, a man: he is an *ideal* man, a Christlike human who comes to human form with the authority of God. Perhaps, says Arthur, he and Guinevere will meet hereafter in heaven (ll. 557–561), and at this point we realize that this, not earth, is the proper sphere for Arthur's actions.

Among the many charges of inconsistency in the *Idylls* one of the chief is that in the final idyll Arthur seems to forget that adultery and the irresponsible quest for the Holy Grail have been primarily the causes for the decay of his kingdom. The answer to this is, I think, that Arthur does not forget: seeing adulterous sin and the Grail quest as but symptoms of the decay of his ideals, Arthur finally half

realizes that he himself has been responsible for the failure
of his ideals. "I perish by this people which I made," he
states. He has destroyed the very social order which he had
created. His knights and their glorious deeds have proved to
him his work, and in their failure he fails. By his power
"That bow'd the will" ("The Passing of Arthur," ll. 290–
291) he had sought to know himself and to prove himself in
his people. With their denial of his authority he no longer
is sure of his identity:

> on my heart hath fallen
> Confusion, till I know not what I am,
> Nor whence I am, nor whether I be a king;
> Behold, I seem but king among the dead.
>
> (ll. 143–146)

If my interpretation of the *Idylls of the King* be allowed,
these lines, which most commentators have found central to
the main theme of the poem but seemingly inexplicable,
take on new meaning. Arthur's failure results from the
frustration of self, a final inability to project fully his will
on his people. Seeing his knights as but the projection of
himself, the instruments by which the self and the self's
values are known, he realizes that with the failure of these
agents of his will he too must fail.

At the end Arthur learns that the world is impregnable to
morality. As the agent of God, the Absolute Self, he had
come to redeem the world: "For I being simple, thought to
work His will" (l. 22); but the world is irredeemable, and
so "all my realm / Reels back into the beast, and is no more"
(ll. 25–26). Like the Arthur of *In Memoriam,* he appeared

ere the times were ripe; the earth is not yet ready to receive her saints.

The ultimate meaning of Tennyson's *Idylls* lies, I believe, in the paradox of Arthur. He set out to found a society based on freedom, but to his sorrow he learned that he could not create a free man. His will simultaneously desired social freedom and social slavery. For a while Arthur is content with self-deception, but in the end he can no longer avoid recognizing his deceptions and the unresolvable paradox of reality. For the imposition of his heroic authority, his will, upon reality meant the denial to others of their own moral responsibility. Arthur stands, finally, in moral terms, as both the hero and the villain of the *Idylls of the King*.

In his study of Greek tragedy Nietzsche discovered that the tragic hero is always justified, because he issues forth from a realm outside the world of moral values. The hero, the mask of God, takes on individuality in order to manifest the values of his heavenly domain through moral action. But, says Nietzsche, the action always ends in crime, for the values of the hero present themselves as evil since they clash with conventional moral categories:

> We may express the Janus face, at once Dionysiac and Apollonian, of the Aeschylean Prometheus in the following formula: "Whatever exists is both just and unjust, and equally justified in both." [6]

The paradox is finally resolved by the destruction of the

[6] *The Birth of Tragedy*, trans. Francis Golffing (Garden City, N. Y., 1956), p. 65.

hero, which is his fate in the moral world, and his return to the realm of pure value where he is justified.

What Nietzsche found true of Greek tragedy is, I think, likewise true of the *Idylls of the King*. In terms of moral considerations Arthur must meet with destruction; he is guilty of violation of the freedom of others, and like any perpetrator of violence he must pay for his misdeed. This is the "Apollonian" judgment upon him. Yet in terms of the "Dionysiac" point of view he is to be applauded as the highest manifestation of the eternal will, the will of the Absolute Self. "God fulfills himself in many ways," Arthur tells Bedivere, "Lest one good custom should corrupt the world" (ll. 409–410). This is, Tennyson implies, the paradox of reality.

In the *Idylls* Tennyson retreats, as I have said and will discuss further in the next chapter, from the optimistic view of life adumbrated in *In Memoriam*. He returns, I believe, to something closely approximating the pessimistic view enunciated in "The Lady of Shalott." In that early poem, it will be remembered, the self is called from its isolation in the tower by the love of something in the world of reality. Yet in this very advance from shadows to realities the self is destroyed: the Lady is transformed and dies when she comes into contact with the outside world. In the *Idylls* Tennyson, in a larger context, implies once again that the antagonism between the tower of self and the city of society is too great and cannot be overcome. On earth there is but constant war between good and evil:

Evolution ever climbing after some ideal good,
And Reversion ever dragging Evolution in the mud.
                    ("Locksley Hall Sixty Years After")

Arthur does not redeem the world because the world is irredeemable. Only the savior is saved. Arthur is allowed entry into the paradise of Avilion because he has brought forth from the innermost recesses of self an affirmation of value and realized its insufficiency *vis à vis* external reality. In knowing that the world cannot be saved and in facing its terrors the self has its victory.

Finally, I should like to suggest how the interpretation of the *Idylls* which I have set forth helps to explain something about the structure of the individual idylls. In the beginning, in the first of the idylls of "The Round Table," the technique is that of straightforward narration. "Gareth and Lynette" begins with Gareth's leaving home, establishing himself at Camelot, and going on the quest with Lynette; all of this is presented in chronological sequence. In "The Marriage of Geraint" we find the flash-back technique, a frame enclosing the main story of the idyll. "Geraint and Enid" picks up with the frame and proceeds once again in normal time sequence. "Balin and Balan" is more complex in form: we begin with the refusal of Pellam to send his tribute before we are introduced to the Balin story. "Merlin and Vivien" is more complex still: the idyll opens with Merlin and Vivien at Broceliande, then switches to Vivien at Mark's court, continues with an account of Vivien at Camelot—all this before we get to the story proper. The next five idylls, beginning with "Lancelot and Elaine" and ending with "Guinevere," are structurally very complicated. In these there is little continuous narrative flow; rather, there is constant backing and filling, a disruption of chronological narration.

The reason for the increasing complication in form of the ten idylls constituting "The Round Table" is, I believe, that this complexity symbolizes the frustration of Arthur in working his will and fulfilling his ideals. What we find, especially in "The Holy Grail" and "The Last Tournament," is the decay of the King's Order indicated by the "broken music" of the narrative flow. The tensions emanating from the guilt, emotional dependency, and failure of the principal actors in these idylls are thus embodied in the very structure of the poem.

IV

The hero: The enlivener of history

With its lesson that the world is irredeemable the *Idylls of the King* seems to reflect much of the pessimism of nineteenth-century philosophy. Indeed, the pattern of Tennyson's thought fits remarkably well into the pattern of the century's intellectual history. To an earlier generation the French Revolution had seemed to herald Utopia. "Bliss was it in that dawn to be alive," wrote Wordsworth, "And to be young was very Heaven!" But when the Revolution failed, all life seemed to have gone out of the universe. This was the period, says Wordsworth, when

> *I lost*
> *All feeling of conviction, and, in fine,*
> *Sick, wearied out with contrarieties,*
> *Yielded up moral questions in despair.*
>
> (*The Prelude*, XI, 108–109, 302–305)

This was the time when Mephistopheles had apparently triumphed and every Faust was in despair.

Just as an earlier generation had placed its faith in revolution, so did a later generation, among whom Tennyson must be numbered, put its faith in evolution. If we can trust *In Memoriam* as a document accurately reflecting the poet's own ideals and aspirations, Tennyson invites us to see a forward-moving design controlling the evolutionary process:

> *Contemplate all this work of Time,*
> *The giant laboring in his youth;*
> *Nor dream of human love and truth,*
> *As dying Nature's earth and lime;*
>
> *But trust that those we call the dead*
> *Are breathers of an ampler day*
> *For ever nobler ends.*

(CXVIII)

In his elegy he postulated the climax of history in the "Christ that is to be," who would surely evolve if biological evolution were accompanied by moral development. The eventual evolution of the Christlike man is the "one far-off divine event, / To which the whole creation moves" (Epilogue). Here Tennyson fell in with the progressive thought stemming from the Enlightenment and reflected in the young Wordsworth and, later, in the writings of Macaulay and the Utilitarians. Time brings the greater man, "Not in vain the distance beacons," so

> *Forward, forward let us range,*
> *Let the great world spin for ever down the ringing grooves*
> *of change.*

("Locksley Hall")

Such pronouncements were, however, the dicta of a poet working himself out of subjective involvement in grief, of a man considering himself in relationship to others and not others in relationship to him and to each other. In other words, *In Memoriam* is "the way of a soul," the poem of a man realizing himself; it is not the way of souls, a poem about men in society. After the experience of writing *In Memoriam* and after, as Laureate, he became the official poetic voice of Britain, Tennyson turned his attention from man in isolation to man in society and devoted an increasingly large part of his poetry to political and social concerns. From his study of what Carlyle called the condition of England, he came more and more to question the progressive ideas enunciated in *In Memoriam*.

For one thing, evolutionary doctrine was, prior to the publication of the elegy in 1850, a matter of concern only among the well-read. But in the 1850's when, *inter alia*, Herbert Spencer supported the economic doctrine of *laissez faire* with analogies drawn from biological evolution and Charles Darwin published the first of his most important works, evolution came to be a topic of casual conversation. Capitalists of even modest learning called upon suppor from evolutionary theory to sanction "free enterprise" and to justify "survival of the fittest" as prevailing "naturally" in economics as well as in nature. "Nature red in tooth and claw," a phrase used by the "I" in *In Memoriam* to describe his fears of a hostile universe, became only a few years later in Tennyson's poetry the image of competitive society. "For nature is one with rapine," the speaker in "Maud" cries,

> *a harm no preacher can heal;*
> *The Mayfly is torn by the swallow, the*
> *sparrow spear'd by the shrike,*
> *And the whole little wood where I sit*
> *is a world of plunder and prey.*

(Pt. I, 123–125)

Secondly, while Tennyson in *In Memoriam* accepted change as purposeful, in the fifties and sixties he feared that change in itself was being regarded as a good in itself. Never so ardent a revolutionary as his friend John Sterling, or as Arthur Hallam for that matter, Tennyson, after the abortive Torrijos episode in 1830 and the rick burnings and disorders attendant upon passage of the first Reform Bill, came more and more to believe in the Burkean ideal of *gradual* change:

> *So let the change which comes be free*
> *To ingroove itself with that which flies,*
> *And work, a joint of state, that plies*
> *Its office, moved with sympathy.*

("Love thou thy land")

What he came to fear was that a violent revolution, not gradual evolution, would shake to pieces, perhaps even in his own lifetime, the civilization which he knew. "All ages are ages of transition," he said, "but this is an awful moment of transition." Again, "When I see society vicious and the poor starving in great cities, I feel that it is a mighty wave of evil passing over the world, but that there will be yet some new and strange development, which I shall not live to see" (*Memoir*, II, 337).

The expanding economy of industrial society was vitiating

the old loyalties and allegiances. When in *In Memoriam* he sought a metaphor to express personal loyalty, what came to mind was the relationship between master and servants:

> *The lesser griefs that may be said,*
>   *That breathe a thousand tender vows,*
>   *Are but as servants in a house*
> *Where lies the master newly dead;*
>
> *Who speak their feeling as it is,*
>   *And weep the fulness from the mind.*
>   *'It will be hard,' they say, 'to find*
> *Another service such as this.'*

(XX)

By the time of "Maud," however, this domestic relationship has become entirely corrupted:

> *I keep but a man and a maid, ever ready to slander and steal;*
> *I know it, and smile a hard-set smile, like a stoic, or like*
> *A wiser epicurean, and let the world have its way.*

(Pt. I, ll. 120–122)

Tennyson had come to believe like his own hero in "Locksley Hall" that his was a time in which "the individual withers, and the world is more and more." Even the most primal of relationships has been debased and replaced by (as Carlyle called it) "the cash nexus": "a Mammonite mother kills her babe for a burial fee" ("Maud," Pt. I, l. 45).

Tennyson's talks with Carlyle and Kingsley and Maurice impressed upon him further the evils resulting from the doctrine of *laissez faire*. They showed him how, in a nation of church-going people, it was Mammon and not God that was worshipped. As Kingsley described the situation, "our churches and chapels are crowded on Sundays by people whose souls are set, the whole week through, upon gain and nothing but gain." [1] Tennyson feared, perhaps even more than Matthew Arnold, the consequences of religious decay throughout all classes of society. For whatever his views of orthodox Christianity, he was convinced that the Christian story—whether it be mythic, as he hints in Lyric XXXVI of *In Memoriam*, or literally true—is still the "creed of creeds." And undoubtedly Christianity's traditional insistence on Original Sin did much to persuade him, after the period of *In Memoriam*, of the truth of Christian theology to human experience.

Finally, Tennyson's study of history militated against the optimism of *In Memoriam*. "What is it all," the speaker asks concerning earth's history in "Vastness," "but a trouble of ants in the gleam of a million million of suns?" The poet became convinced, as the cyclical imagery in the *Idylls* suggests, that in spite of all the varieties of special circumstances and manners and customs there is everywhere the same humanity—mankind flawed, no sooner rising than falling. The pattern of history, he learned, is one of endless cycles. "Chaos, Cosmos! Cosmos, Chaos!" says the speaker in "Locksley Hall Sixty Years After"; this is what one learns from reading "the wide world's annals." The motto of history therefore should be *Eadem, sed aliter*. "Throughout and everywhere the true symbol of nature is the circle,"

[1] Charles Kingsley, *Westminster Sermons* (London, 1874), pp. 293–294.

wrote Schopenhauer many years earlier, "because it is the schema or type of recurrence." [2]

But if history is only a relentless series of cycles in which, as the "I" in "Locksley Hall Sixty Years After" says, reversion drags down what has evolved, what is the justification of life? Tennyson would never have agreed with Schopenhauer that the thwarting of the life process is man's highest goal on earth. On the contrary, he maintains time and again that the purpose of life is to give life—to "Have power on this dark land to lighten it, / And power on this dead world to make it live" ("The Coming of Arthur," ll. 92–93). The temporal sphere as Tennyson sees it is a vale of soul-making which builds up credit for the soul in the world beyond. Though "deed and song alike are swept / Away, and all in vain / As far as man can see," still

> *The man remains, and whatsoe'er*
> *He wrought of good or brave*
> *Will mould him thro' the cycle-year*
> *That dawns behind the grave.*
> (Epilogue to "The Charge of the Heavy Brigade")

Yet, caught in the flux of history, how is man to know what to believe and what deeds to perform? Creeds and philosophies come and go, and the world cannot be understood by old outmoded ones. There is, Tennyson implies, one fixed point in this constant revolution—and that is the great man. In the hero, who is the highest product of the evolutionary process, mankind finds an instrument of prog-

[2] Quoted by William Wallace, *Life of Schopenhauer* (London, n.d.), p. 97.

ress and a justification of life. For the great man comes into time and space with a special kind of authority.

The first of these heroes of history in Tennyson's poetry we find in *In Memoriam,* where, as I suggested in the preceding chapter, Hallam is made a type of Christ on earth and lives on in bliss as part of the Divine. The speaker in "Maud," seeing only chaos in the world about him, prays that a great man might come to reorganize society:

> *Ah God, for a man with heart, head, hand,*
> *Like some of the simple great ones gone*
> *For ever and ever by,*
> *One still strong man in a blatant land,*
> *Whatever they call him—what care I?—*
> *Aristocrat, democrat, autocrat—one*
> *Who can rule and dare not lie!*
>
> (Pt. I, ll. 389–395)

A suggestion of this concept of the heroic redeemer can be discerned in the "Ode on the Death of the Duke of Wellington," where the Duke is said to have given himself over to "the long self-sacrifice of life," to duty and to the obeying of God's command in leading his fellow men. The Duke served as example of what man should be and he demonstrated by his life that time is not meaningless change:

> *For tho' the Giant Ages heave the hill*
> *And break the shore, and evermore*
> *Make and break, and work their will,*
> *Tho' world on world in myriad myriads roll*
> *Round us, each with different powers,*
> *And other forms of life than ours,*
> *What know we greater than the soul?*

By "soul" here Tennyson presumably means the great man, for the very next line is "On God and Godlike men we build our trust." The Iron Duke, having fulfilled his earthly duties, has earned his right into heaven along with the other great men of history, and like Hallam he lives on with God.

By identifying his heroes with Christ, Tennyson sought, I believe, to suggest the supernatural authority of these "Godlike men." His identification of Arthur in the *Idylls* with Christ is so obvious to any reader familiar with the New Testament that the resemblances need hardly be pointed out. Quite early, of course, the Arthurian legend became confused with the Christian story. This is partly the reason, I think, why Tennyson was attracted to Arthur as a subject for a long poem. But besides such likenesses to Christ as the mystery surrounding his birth, his twelve "disciple" knights, his mysterious death, and his promise to come again, Tennyson put into Arthur's mouth whole phrases and sentences drawn from the words of Jesus. Surely no Western reader can go through the lines of "The Passing of Arthur," say, without recognizing Biblical parallels in such lines as "My God, thou hast forgotten me in my death" (l. 27). This is but one example; there are numerous more. Why, we must ask ourselves, why has Tennyson gone to such lengths to underscore the similarity of Arthur to Jesus? The answer can only be that he wished to make King Arthur, as he made Arthur Hallam, a type of Christ.

Tennyson seems to have fully assimilated the nineteenth-century doctrine regarding history as an organic growth arranging itself in epochs and repeating itself in cycles. In this view society is regarded as organic and, like other organisms, is subject to decay. Periodically there is catastrophe followed by a fresh start, at which time individuals and societies experience rebirth. This is the situation at the beginning of the *Idylls of the King*. Roman vitality and order in Britain are exhausted: the petty kingdoms constantly war; the land is harried by a heathen host; the wilderness encroaches upon cultivated soil; and "the beast was more and more, / But man was less and less" ("The Coming of Arthur," ll. 5–10). Then comes Arthur, who serves the dual function of creating a new society and providing a pattern for others to imitate. Society is reborn: the petty kingdoms are united; Camelot is built; and the people are revitalized. Thus in the early idylls we find joy on the part of all the people in the new creation: they reverence their king and honor his commands and "Were all one will" ("The Coming of Arthur," l. 515). Tennyson commented "that the great resolve (to ennoble and spiritualize mankind) is kept so long as all work in obedience to the highest and holiest law within them" (*Memoir*, II, 130)—that is, so long as they reverence their king.

Tennyson's veneration of the great man, it seems highly likely, owes more than a little to the influence of Carlyle. The two men, as is well known, were good friends. Furthermore, we have it on excellent authority that Tennyson was disposed to agree with Carlyle on the subject of heroes and hero-worship.[3] This is not surprising when we recall that

[3] Wilfrid Ward, "Talks with Tennyson," *New Review*, XV (1896), 80–81.

FROM THE GREAT DEEP 104

Tennyson maintained, "I believe in God, not from what I see in Nature, but from what I see in man." [4] With Carlyle the poet evidently agreed that Christianity is "the highest instance of Hero-worship." [5] " 'The Son of Man' was the most tremendous title possible," Tennyson held (*Memoir*, I, 326). Because he "disliked discussion on the Nature of Christ" (*Memoir*, I, 326), we are never told, either in his poetry or in his biography, what he thought of the divinity of Christ; in almost every reference to Him, we see only the poet's belief in Jesus as the great, perhaps perfect, man, and we learn that "our highest view of God must be more or less anthropomorphic" (*Memoir*, I, 311). Tennyson was singularly reticent about his own belief in God, refusing at times even to name Him—more or less in the manner of Carlyle, who maintained, "The greatest of all Heroes is One—whom we do not name here" (*Heroes*, p. 15); for, says his son, "He dreaded the dogmatism of sects and rash definitions of God" (*Memoir*, I, 311). "But," he insisted, "take away belief in the self-conscious personality of God and you take away the backbone of the world" (*Memoir*, I, 311).

In Arthur, as in Christ, God manifests Himself again. Like Carlyle's heroes Arthur is king by right of power, not by right of birth. It was to make this very point that Tennyson arranges, in the first idyll, to becloud the legitimacy of Arthur's claim to the throne. "Wilt thou leave / Thine easeful biding here, and risk thine all," his mother asks Gareth,

4 Quoted by C. F. G. Masterman, *Tennyson as a Religious Teacher* (Boston, 1900), p. 149.
5 *On Heroes, Hero-Worship, and The Heroic in History* (London, 1901), p. 17.

"Life, limbs, for one that is not proven king?" Gareth replies:

> *Not proven, who swept the dust of ruin'd Rome*
> *From off the threshold of the realm, and crush'd*
> *The idolaters, and made the people free?*
> *Who should be king save him who makes us free?*
> ("Gareth and Lynette," ll. 125–127, 133–136)

Not by inheritance, then, but as the powerful arm working God's will is the hero recognized.

Under Arthur's command the knights "slew the beast, and fell'd / The forest, letting in the sun" ("The Coming of Arthur," ll. 59–60). The light image here is entirely appropriate. For, in Carlyle's words, the great man is "the living light fountain," the "light which enlightens, which has enlightened the darkness of the world; and this not as a kindled light only, but rather as a natural luminary shining by the gift of Heaven; a flowing light-fountain . . . of native original insight, of manhood and heroic nobleness; —in whose radiance all souls feel that it is well with them" (*Heroes,* p. 4). The hero is then a gift of heaven—"the Soul of a Man actually sent down from the skies with a God's message for us" (*Heroes,* p. 52)—whose essential quality is original insight and whose service is to teach the divine mystery. Thus it is he who sees the inner Reality of the world, while the ordinary man is deluded by the appearances of a partially or even faultily apprehended universe. For this very reason, therefore, in the *Idylls of the King* it is right that the knights sing:

> *The King will follow Christ, and we the King,*
> *In whom high God hath breathed a secret thing.*
> ("The Coming of Arthur," ll. 499–500)

And because they have, as Carlyle said, a duty to follow the highest manifestation of the Will of the Universe, the knights rightly swear the vows of utter loyalty enjoined upon them by the King, promising

> *To reverence the King, as if he were*
> *Their conscience, and their conscience as their King.*
> ("Guinevere," ll. 465–466)

As the knights of the Round Table more and more disregard their king, when they lose what Carlyle calls "transcendent admiration of a Great Man" (*Heroes*, p. 14), the skies darken over Camelot. Creeping materialism infects society and leads to spiritual paralysis; men become absorbed in the semblances of the world and foreswear their vows of loyalty to the Divine as manifested in the person of the King. Tennyson, as paraphrased by his son Hallam, explained it as poison spreading through the whole community:

> In some natures, even among those who would "rather die than doubt," it breeds suspicion and want of trust in God and man. Some loyal souls are wrought to madness against the world. Others, and some among the highest intellects, become the slaves of the evil which is at first half-disdained. Tender natures sink under the blight, that which is of the highest in them working their death. And in some, as faith declines, religion turns from practical goodness and holiness to superstition.
>
> (*Memoir*, II, 131)

When in the penultimate idyll of "The Round Table" we find Tristram scoffing at the vows which he had sworn to Arthur, we know that Modred was indeed correct in thinking, "The time is hard at hand" ("Pelleas and Ettarre," l. 597).

The growing scepticism on the part of the knights is a sign that the vitality of society is waning. But, says Carlyle, "the decay of old ways of believing" is "the preparation afar off for new better and wider ways,—an inevitable thing. . . . We will understand that destruction of old *forms* is not destruction of everlasting *substances;* that Scepticism, as sorrowful and hateful as we see it, is not an end but a beginning" (*Heroes,* p. 203). Tennyson evidently agrees with Carlyle when he puts these words into the mouth of Arthur:

> *The old order changeth, yielding place to new,*
> *And God fulfils himself in many ways,*
> *Lest one good custom should corrupt the world.*
>
> ("The Passing of Arthur," ll. 408–410)

What could these lines mean other than that the failing of this organism is but the herald of a new society which will be vitalized by another such man as Arthur?

In this context let us examine the fire or light motif, which is closely allied to the water imagery discussed in an earlier chapter. Throughout the *Idylls* Arthur is described in terms of brilliant light. In "The Coming of Arthur" the child is borne from the sea in a wave of flame. When Merlin picks up the babe, both "the child and he were clothed in fire" (ll. 381–389). Lancelot acknowledges Arthur as king when,

he says, "the fire of God / Descends upon thee in the battle-
field" (ll. 127–129). When Arthur enjoins his vows upon the
knights, they rise "dazed, as one who wakes / Half-blinded
at the coming of a light" ("The Coming of Arthur," ll. 264–
265). At his marriage, when "The sun of May descended on
their King" and the city was "all on fire / With sun," the
knights sing:

> Blow, for our Sun is mighty in his May!
> Blow, for our Sun is mightier day by day!
>
> (ll. 461, 478–479, 496–497)

In the ten idylls of "The Round Table" Arthur is constantly spoken of in terms of brilliant, often blinding, light.
Gareth refers to him as "great Sun of Glory" ("Gareth and
Lynette," l. 22). In excusing her sin, Guinevere compares
Arthur to the sun, saying, "But who can gaze upon the sun
in heaven?" ("Lancelot and Elaine," l. 123). Tristram describes the King thus:

> His hair, a sun that ray'd from off a brow
> Like hill-snow high in heaven, the steel-blue eyes,
> The golden beard that clothed his lips with light.
>
> ("The Last Tournament," ll. 661–663)

Finally, to give but one more example, Guinevere's dream
of the end is of herself standing "On some vast plain before
a setting sun," and her last sight of her husband is of a giant
figure in a blazing steam of fire ("Guinevere," ll. 76, 591–
595).

The attributes of Arthur, furthermore, are described in

terms of light. Excalibur has a "blade so bright / That men are blinded by it" ("The Coming of Arthur," ll. 299–300). The sight of Camelot dazzles Gareth and his companions when they see flash the summit of the high city ("Gareth and Lynette," (l. 189). The statue of Arthur made by Merlin has a crown and wings which flame and assure the people that they have a king ("The Holy Grail," ll. 241–245). The rays of light falling on the three queens near Arthur's throne are "Flame-color, vert, and azure" ("The Coming of Arthur," l. 274).

This imagery is fairly obvious, and I mention it only because it has a direct bearing on the end of the *Idylls*. At the close of "The Passing of Arthur" Bedivere sees Arthur "vanish into light." And, the narrator tells us, "the new sun rose bringing the new year." Since Tennyson has throughout the twelve idylls so carefully established the image of the sun in relationship to Arthur, what are we to make of this last line of the *Idylls of the King*? Does it indeed mean that Arthur will come again? The answer to this question reveals, I think, a great deal about Tennyson's philosophy of history and his concept of the hero in history.

Societies may fail and heroes may pass, Tennyson implies, but their passing does not mean that all Godhood is forever withdrawn from the universe. For the hero will come again. Pray for me, Arthur tells Bedivere, "let thy voice / Rise like a fountain for me night and day"—which admonition I understand to mean that Bedivere should pray for the return of Arthur, or a man like him. For, says Arthur, are men any better than animals who "lift not hands of prayer / Both for themselves and those who call them friend?" ("The Passing of Arthur," ll. 415–421). So Arthur passes on to the island-valley of Avilion, "Where I will heal me of my grievous wound," in order to return refreshed. And as he vanishes into light the sun rises bringing the new year, clearly indicating, I believe, that the hero will come again to clear the waste and enlighten the land.

When in the epilogue "To the Queen" Tennyson spoke of his idylls as a tale "shadowing Sense at war with Soul," he meant exactly what he said. To see the *Idylls* only as the presentation of the downfall of a kingdom resulting from the sin of adultery is, in my estimation, to take a partial view of this very complex philosophical poem. Certainly the poem treats of the harm resulting when pleasures of the flesh, "Sense," become paramount and dominate or obliterate the spiritual values of society, "Soul." Indeed, in this respect *Idylls of the King* is something of a prototype for such modern stories as *La Dolce Vita* which show the degenerative effects of an easy eroticism. Tennyson tells us quite clearly, however, that his work but *shadows* this theme, by which I understand him to mean that this is a theme treated not only allegorically but also secondarily. On a higher and primary level the *Idylls* demonstrates dramatically what happens when a community denies its obligations to the Ideal—the Ideal "closed in real man," that is, as embodied in Arthur. Perhaps nowhere is this brought out so openly or so well as in "Guinevere." At the end the Queen becomes aware that Arthur not only was her husband but also represented the highest ideals of society. "It was my duty to have loved the highest," she belatedly realizes. "We needs must love the highest when we see it" (ll. 652, 655). Proper veneration of the hero, the man sent from God and thus embodying the highest attributes, is, Tennyson implies by pronouncing upon Guinevere no harsher judgment, difficult. As Carlyle says, "It is a thing forever changing, this of Hero-worship: different in each age, difficult to do well in any age." Yet, Tennyson would agree with Carlyle, "Indeed, the heart of the whole business of the age, one may say, is to do it well" (*Heroes*, p. 52).

On one level, the "message" of *Idylls of the King* is that present civilization, which has "much less of the old reverence and chivalrous feeling . . . than there used to be' (*Memoir*, II, 337), will succumb to "The darkness of that battle in the west / Where all of high and holy dies away" unless it recognizes allegiance to an ideal. Hero worship is, however, still possible in modern life. Near the close of his life Tennyson said, "I am old and I may be wrong, for this generation has assuredly some spirit of chivalry. We see it in acts of heroism by land and sea, in fights against the slave trade, in our Arctic voyages, in philanthropy, etc. The truth is that the wave advances and recedes. I tried in my 'Idylls' to teach men these things, and the need of the Ideal" (*Memoir*, II, 337).

Ultimately, the *Idylls of the King* is not the pessimistic work that it at first appears. Though we witness *Götterdämmerung* we also in the symbolic close are presented with the dawn betokening a new life. Tennyson's own gloss on these last lines is as follows: "From (the dawn) the East, whence

FROM THE GREAT DEEP 112

have sprung all the great religions of the world." [6] If I interpret this gloss correctly, the symbolic close of the *Idylls* suggests that though the Christian hero, like Arthur, may perish, there is ever imminent another kind of hero who will come forth in another guise to justify mortal existence.

[6] *The Works of Tennyson, With Notes by the Author,* ed. Hallam, Lord Tennyson (New York, 1939), p. 964.

V

Eros and Agape

If the hero with a divine mission cannot redeem the world, how then may the world be saved? This is the question implicitly confronting the actors in the *Idylls of the King* when they doubt the authority of the King. Years earlier in the nineteenth century when it became impossible for the thinking man to accept unquestioningly an inherited world view, the same question had been posed and tentatively answered: redemption comes only through love. "By love subsists / All lasting grandeur, by pervading love; / That gone, we are as dust," Wordsworth had written in *The Prelude* (Bk. XIV); Goethe's Faust had been able to re-enter the great world and participate in its actions by means of his love for Gretchen; Wagner's Flying Dutchman had found respite from the curse imposed upon him through Senta's devotion—the idea is found in many Romantic works. Not surprisingly this was one of the few transcendental concepts of Romanticism that filtered down to the mass public. By mid-century the notion of redemption through love had become the basis of a vast body of literature, leading finally to a sanctification of love. Coventry Patmore's *The Angel in the House,* for example, attests to the vitality of the concept. Eros was praised as a god.

It is customary, I believe, to include Tennyson among these praisers of love, to categorize him as the laureate of the domestic affections. In my opinion this is a false view of the poet. For Tennyson never praises married, or any other kind of, love as an end in itself. With Wordsworth he recognizes that "Unless this love by a still higher love / Be hallowed," unless it be "By heaven inspired," it is "but delight how pitiable" (*The Prelude,* Bk. XIV). Tennyson saw, to recall M. de Rougemont's observation,[1] that when Eros is made a god it ends by being a demon. As Ortega y Gasset has said,

> The ideology of recent times has lost cosmological inspiration and has become almost exclusively psychological. Refinements in the psychology of love, by multiplying subtle casuistry, have drawn away our attention from this cosmic dimension, which is elemental to love. . . . We must not forget, however, that the multiform history of our loves, with all their complications and incidents, lives finally from that elemental, cosmic force, which our psyche—primitive or refined, simple or complex, from one century to another— merely administers and models in varied ways.[2]

This is the lesson Tennyson sought to demonstrate in the *Idylls of the King,* which may justly be regarded as a series

1 Denis de Rougemont, *Passion and Society,* trans. Montgomery Belgion (London, 1956), p. 312.
2 José Ortega y Gasset, *On Love: Aspects of a Single Theme,* trans. Toby Talbot (New York, 1957), p. 37.

of love stories. But before we begin an examination of the
Idylls on this subject, I think we had best recall again some
of Tennyson's earlier pronouncements on love.

In his earliest poetry Tennyson was preoccupied with the
self in isolation, aware almost to the point of utter despair of
the gulf between the self and the external world. In so early
an endeavor as *The Devil and the Lady,* written at the age
of fourteen, he asks:

> *O suns and spheres and stars and belts and systems,*
> *Are ye or are ye not?*
> *Are ye realities or semblances*
> *Of that which men call real?*
> *Are ye true substance? are ye anything*
> *Except delusive shows. . . ?*

(II, i)

The answer which he found for bridging the gulf is, as I
suggested in the third chapter, love: only love can "rend the
veil in twain" ("Love," sonnet ii) which separates the self
and all the living universe. Love alone is the bond which
unites the diverse consciousness of men. Love, Tennyson
learned, affirms an object, asserts its right to exist; love says,
in effect, that the object is worthy of existence—and this not
a judicial recognition of a right but a decision which means
participation in and enactment of that right. Thus through
love the self is able to escape from its own prison.

Love, then, is the reality of the universe. God is Love:
this is the basic fact of man's existence, Tennyson says.
"Love is and was my Lord and King," the "I" asserts in *In
Memoriam* (CXXVI); and at the close of his life the poet

reaffirms his belief in "That Love which is and was / My father, and my brother, and my God" ("Doubt and Prayer"). When we love we approach nearest to God, and in the act of loving we offer up our praise to Him. A sin against love, therefore, is a sin against God. A man who rejects love is unable to perform a moral act, has, in other words, made a shambles of his life:

> *And he that shuts Love out, in turn shall be*
> *Shut out from Love, and on her threshold lie*
> *Howling in outer darkness.*
> (Introductory Stanzas to "The Palace of Art")

This is the lesson of almost every one of Tennyson's poems. The soul in "The Palace of Art" fell into a state of dread and horror because she had devoted herself to beauty and neglected love. In *The Princess* Ida's ideal is wrecked because she had left no place in her scheme for love. In "Aylmer's Field" the pride of lineage triumphed over the right of love and resulted in a dreadful punishment.

Poem after poem recounts the joys of domestic bliss and the spiritual enrichment offered by married love. But sentimental though such idylls as "The Miller's Daughter" are, none of them treats domestic love in quite the same way as Patmore's *The Angel in the House* or any one of hundreds of popular novels. For Tennyson never maintains that virtue lies in giving all for love or that for love the world is well lost. On the contrary, he insists that love is worthy, or valid, only when it is based on something higher than love, only when it serves as a stimulus to right moral action. Duty,

which is "loved of Love," demands a higher claim than the
fulfillment of earthly love. Ofttimes duty comes "Like Death
betwixt thy dear embrace and mine" ("Love and Duty"),
but its claims must be heeded. And this indeed is what true
love is—a union which means not death to the world but
"more life and fuller" ("The Two Voices"). In this way
alone does love ennoble us and make us greater than what
we have been.

Throughout *In Memoriam* Tennyson reiterates his belief
in love as that part of God in man. It is the one thing which
does not change, the planet in which Hesper and Phosphor
unite (CXXI), but which only grows:

> *My love involves the love before;*
> *My love is vaster passion now;*
> *Tho' mix'd with God and Nature thou,*
> *I seem to love thee more and more.*
>
> (CXXX)

Thus love involves a transcendence of the purely aesthetic
sphere of existence—which dissolves all reality into possibility, to which the moment is everything, and, further,
which is marked by despair and satiety—into a higher sphere,
whose chief principle is morality and obedience to duty.
Tennyson fully comprehended the meaning of Lovelace's
statement to his beloved: "I could not love thee, dear, so
much, / Lov'd I not honour more."

Tennyson praised love, but he also saw its dangers. In
examining the literature of his day he saw that love had
become a substitute for religion. This was, he believed, a

wholly fallacious concept, for, he maintained, "The love of God is the true basis of duty, truth, reverence, loyalty, love, virtue, and work" (*Memoir*, I, 318). Love cannot be considered a substitute for God because without God there can be no love, only the illusion that love exists.

"On God and Godlike men we build our trust," Tennyson was fond of saying (*Memoir*, I, 311). As I have pointed out in the previous chapter Arthur is to be considered the agent of God on earth. It is the duty of those under him to trust in him and follow his example. Yet the way of the Godlike man is difficult, and all too often even those who have sworn allegiance to him are, through deficiency of will, unable to keep to his path. When they falter, Tennyson implies, they are inclined to transfer their allegiance elsewhere, to lose themselves in another undertaking and in other experiences. This, for the most part, is what the lovers do in the *Idylls*.

Regarded as a series of romances about lovers, the *Idylls* revolves around Guinevere. Arthur has taken her as his queen because, as man, he must break through the walls of self-hood, and by his love for her realize himself as a living, active soul. "What happiness," he asks, in lines reminiscent of the passage previously quoted from *The Devil and the Lady*,

> What happiness to reign a lonely king,
> Vext—O ye stars that shudder over me,
> O earth that soundest hollow under me,
> Vext with waste dreams? for saving I be join'd
> To her that is the fairest under heaven,
> I seem as nothing in the mighty world,

And cannot will my will nor work my work
Wholly, nor make myself in mine own realm
Victor and lord.

("The Coming of Arthur," ll. 81–89)

But were he joined with her,

Then might we live together as one life,
And reigning with one will in everything
Have power on this dark land to lighten it,
And power on this dead world to make it live.

(ll. 90–93)

He regards marriage as the means to service and to a greater love, for in marriage passion is worshipped not for itself but as the highest value in the ethical sphere. So Arthur and Guinevere are wedded, "Sware at the shrine of Christ a deathless love," and listen to "holy" Dubric's admonition:

Reign ye, and live and love, and make the world
Other, and may thy Queen be one with thee. . . .

("The Coming of Arthur," ll. 471–472)

Tennyson does not tell us how the illicit love between Lancelot and Guinevere began, although we are led to believe that it stemmed from Guinevere's delusion that Lancelot was Arthur when she first saw him; rather, he tells us only of its tragic effects. We never see the lovers happy; in fact, we see them mainly in the background, as guilty presences who have broken their vows to God and the King. In the early idylls we find Guinevere "Lost in sweet dreams, and dreaming of her love" and forgetful of her duties ("The Marriage of Geraint," ll. 158–159). When we first meet

Lancelot and Guinevere together after her marriage, he too is lost in dreams. Guinevere remonstrates with him for having passed her by without greeting: "ye stand, fair lord, as in a dream." Lancelot replies:

> *Yea—for a dream. Last night methought I saw*
> *That maiden Saint who stands with lily in hand*
> *In yonder shrine. All round her prest the dark,*
> *And all the light upon her silver face*
> *Flow'd from the spiritual lily that she held.*
> *Lo! these her emblems drew mine eyes—away;*
> *For see, how perfect-pure!*

"Sweeter to me," the Queen answers,

> *this garden rose*
> *Deep-hued and many-folded! sweeter still*
> *The wild-wood hyacinth and the bloom of May!*
> *Prince, we have ridden before among the flowers*
> *In those fair days—not all as cool as these,*
> *Tho' season-earlier. Art thou sad? or sick?*
> *Our noble King will send thee his own leech—*
> *Sick? or for any matter anger'd at me?*

Then, the poet tells us, "Lancelot lifted his large eyes; they dwelt / Deep-tranced on hers, and could not fall" ("Balin and Balan," ll. 253–273). Already we see the lover willing to forsake the demands of the religious life for the claims of love.

The idylls that follow show the decay of Lancelot as a knight of the Round Table. In the beginning of "Lancelot and Elaine" we see him lying to his king—who insists that "Man's word is God in man"—and engaging in a kind of deceit, out of the promptings of love, to win the tournament. Furthermore, the guilt which proceeds from his illicit love for Guinevere has coarsened not only his moral sensibilities but also his appearance:

> *The great and guilty love he bare the Queen,*
> *In battle with the love he bare his lord,*
> *Had marr'd his face, and mark'd it ere his time.*

Moreover, it drives him into paroxysms of agony and eventually, in "The Holy Grail," to madness:

> *His mood was often like a fiend, and rose*
> *And drove him into wastes and solitudes*
> *For agony, who was yet a living soul.*
> ("Lancelot and Elaine," ll. 244–246, 250–252)

As we read further in the *Idylls* the more we become aware of the fact that the alliance between Lancelot and Guinevere is one of passion and not of true love. For the very nature of passion is somehow to keep going, to meet obstructions in order to overcome them and once again experience itself for its own sake. This, of course, explains the psychology of jealousy, which is an inability to accept another human being for his own sake, his own limitations and reality. Passion glorifies itself and the object through which it finds expression, and unable to maintain itself in this intensity it passes from raptures to mere sensation. Finding it impossible to enjoy what reality has given him, the lover of passion is likewise unable to believe in the constancy of the beloved. Tennyson shows us this jealousy taking posses-

sion of Guinevere. Upon hearing that Lancelot had worn a
lady's emblem upon his helmet into the tournament, she

> Past to her chamber, and there flung herself
> Down on the great King's couch, and writhed upon it,
> And clench'd her fingers till they bit the palm,
> And shriek'd out 'Traitor!' to the unhearing wall,
> Then flash'd into wild tears. . . .
>
>   ("Lancelot and Elaine," ll. 605–609)

And upon his return she charges Lancelot with inconstancy
in a mad rage. But neither Guinevere nor Lancelot, guilty
things though we see them to be, ever wholly loses our
sympathy, for each is very much aware of his guilt and his
sin. Guinevere tells her lover:

>   I for you
> This many a year have done despite and wrong
> To one whom ever in my heart of hearts
> I did acknowledge nobler.

And Lancelot feels the shackles of passion and realizes that
"His honor rooted in dishonor stood, / And faith unfaithful
kept him falsely true" ("Lancelot and Elaine," ll. 1201–1204,
871–872).

Each of the lovers would rationally like to forego his passion. They see the harm it works and wish, never wholeheartedly, however, to be free and let the other go. Lancelot
perceives that jealousy is not love's curse, as he had told the
Queen (l. 1342) but rather "dead love's harsh heir, jealous
pride" (l. 1387). He realizes that he "must break / These

bonds that so defame me," yet he knows that he, passion's slave, cannot do so: "Not without / She wills it—and would I, if she will'd it?" (ll. 1409–1411).

Here Tennyson profoundly explores the nature of erotic love. It means, the poet implies, a complete surrender of the will, without which one is powerless to choose. Thus erotic love can only result in ill to him who, Tennyson says in another poem, "Corrupts the strength of heaven-descended Will, / And ever weaker grows thro' acted crime, / Or seem-ing-genial venial fault, / Recurring and suggesting still" ("Will"). Without will the lover loses, so to speak, his sanity. "Better to die together, to live together unhappily, than to live happily apart," passion cries out. For passion—and I speak here not only of carnal love but of the love which cus-tomarily is designated as Eros—demands total commitment, transcendence of self-regard as well as regard for the world. Thus caught in the snares of passion, Lancelot is unable to break away from that love which he instinctively and rationally realizes demeans him.

The love of Lancelot and Guinevere is like a disease which they want to cure but cannot, for their love is consumed by that which once nourished it. Both, intuiting the shame which must inevitably result, wish to break away, yet even at the very end they find themselves controlled by desire. It is, I think, highly unlikely that they would have ever been able to leave each other unless circumstance, in the person of Modred, had forced them to. As M. de Rougemont has said, man's "desires are intensified and sublimated by the god Eros through being embraced in a single Desire whereby they are abolished. The final goal of the process is to attain what is not life—the death of the body." [3] The very nature of their passion has been a denial of love, which is creative, not destructive. "The children born of thee," Arthur tells Guinevere, "are sword and fire, / Red ruin, and the breaking up of laws" ("Guinevere," ll. 422–423).

In exile the Queen at last fully realizes the extent of her sinfulness. Through Arthur's instruction she is made to see the falseness of her love for Lancelot. Briefly, what the King tells her is this: love endures only when it is predicated on something else. Love, Arthur says, is not a state of being but instead a state of acting: to be in love is not the same as to love. Love is a power granted to man by the grace of God to fulfill his potentialities. Eros, in that it demands a transcendence of self-regard, can be an agent for good: it can become a paradigm of the love which man ought to exercise toward God. Eros becomes evil only when it is, itself, idolized. "I knew," Arthur says,

> Of no more subtle master under heaven
> Than is the maiden passion for a maid,
> Not only to keep down the base in man,
> But teach high thought, and amiable words
> And courtliness, and the desire of fame,
> And love of truth, and all that makes a man.
>
> ("Guinevere," ll. 474–480)

Yet Guinevere and Lancelot have denied this creativity of love. Their passion has been "like a new disease," which

---

[3] *Passion and Society,* p. 67.

Creeps, no precaution used, among the crowd,
Makes wicked lightnings of her eyes, and saps
The fealty of our friends, and stirs the pulse
With devil's leaps, and poisons half the young.
("Guinevere," ll. 516–519)

The King's love, on the other hand, is constant even in adversity. By the nature of her crime the King cannot take Guinevere back as his wife, yet he loves her still. He accepts her limitations, even forgives her, because, possessed of the Godlike in man, he is able to forgive "as Eternal God / Forgives" ("Guinevere," ll. 541–542). He insists that she can expiate her sin and gain true love by loving God, which previously she had not done. For in her pride she had taken, she says,

Full easily all impressions from below,
Would not look up, or half-despised the height
To which I would not or I could not climb—
I thought I could not breathe in that fine air,
That pure severity of perfect light—
I yearn'd for warmth and color which I found
In Lancelot—now I see thee what thou art,
Thou art the highest and most human too,
Not Lancelot, nor another
("Guinevere," ll. 637–645)

Only now in her abasement does she realize that "We needs must love the highest when we see it" (l. 655). So in a life of prayer she seeks to atone for her guilt, and as, we are told, Lancelot died a holy man, so Guinevere dies a holy woman.

Love has proved a delusion to the lovers: instead of a fructification of life it has meant sterility and guilt and shame. The flowers associated with Guinevere's love for Lancelot have in the end become the weeds of death and ruin. For the lovers had abandoned their wills; they forgot that the garden of love must be tended, that the will must hack and prune the weeds and poisonous plants. Eros may be a natural love, the *Idylls* implies, but it can never be justified on purely natural grounds.

It is to Eros as a "natural" god that Tristram turns in "The Last Tournament." In a time when a civilization is waning, when the world seems in need of reform but is seemingly irreformable, men frequently turn to nature as the one source of value because it appears sane and graceful. So Tristram throws his vows to the wind and takes to the woods, just as Balin had done. But worse than Balin, Tristram refuses to recognize any ideal. He is "woodsman of the woods," the harrier of wild beasts who recognizes subservience only to natural law, which does not admit obligation. His rejection of restraint is summed up in his song:

> *Free love—free field—we love but while we may.*
> *The woods are hush'd, their music is no more;*
> *The leaf is dead, the yearning past away.*
> *New leaf, new life—the days of frost are o'er;*
> *New life, new love, to suit the newer day;*
> *New loves are sweet as those that went before.*
> *Free love—free field—we love but while we may.*

(ll. 275-281)

It is fitting that Tristram is the victor in the last tournament because Lancelot is the winner in the first that is presented in the *Idylls*—fitting because Tristram is the counterpart of Lancelot: a Lancelot in strength and daring and, to put it baldly, in adultery, but the opposite of Lancelot in grace and courtesy and conscience. In the first tournament Lancelot is the winner of a diamond, the last of nine, that comes from the crown of a king slain by his brother. Seemingly of such lasting beauty, it and the other diamonds are thrown away by Guinevere in a fit of jealous rage: from death they come and to death, in that they are lost to men, they return—an apt comment on the whole relationship obtaining between Lancelot and Guinevere. But the manner of their being won tells us much about Lancelot: he gained them in honorable combat at a tournament where courtesy and manners prevailed. In the last tournament, however, the prize, a ruby carcanet from a dead child's crown, is won on a field where courtesy and honor are absent. Appropriately it is Lancelot, not the King, who presides at this contest—appropriately because Lancelot has, so to speak, replaced the King as the "ideal" of the kingdom. Although neither Lancelot nor Guinevere can abide the conduct of the knights or the audience at the last tournament, this nevertheless is what their guilty passion has led to. "Crown'd warrant had we for the crowning sin," Tristram tells his beloved (l. 572). In a process of spiritual "devolution" the sin of Lancelot and Guinevere—so tentative, so guilt-ridden, so tragic—has resulted in the mannerlessness and animality of Tristram and the Red Knight.

As with the diamonds of the first tournament, the rubies, the prize of the last tournament, take on complex symbolic value. The clear light of the diamonds, although refractory,

changes to the darker light of the ruby carcanet. Tristram's
dream of the rubies and the two Isolts mordantly symbolizes
the change in values in Camelot:

> *He seem'd to pace the strand of Brittany*
> *Between Isolt of Britain and his bride,*
> *And show'd them both the ruby-chain, and both*
> *Began to struggle for it, till his queen*
> *Graspt it so hard that all her hand was red.*
> *Then cried the Breton, 'Look, her hand is red!*
> *These be no rubies, this is frozen blood,*
> *And melts within her hand—her hand is hot*
> *With ill desires, but this I gave thee, look,*
> *Is all as cool and white as any flower.'*
> *Follow'd a rush of eagle's wings, and then*
> *A whimpering of the spirit of the child,*
> *Because the twain had spoil'd her carcanet.*
>
> (ll. 406–418)

Yet Tristram is as unable to act on the truth of his dream
as Lancelot was unable to act on his in "Balin and Balan."
Caught in the web of desire, he like Lancelot is denied the
power to choose the purer, for he too has resigned his will
to passion—which action, Tennyson suggests by interjecting
the Red Knight episode, can lead only to ruin.

When Isolt is introduced, we are left without any doubt
whatsoever as to the nature of her love. She loves Tristram
because she hates Mark: "My soul," she says to her lover
when he suddenly appears, "I felt my hatred for my Mark /
Quicken within me, and knew that thou wert nigh" (ll. 517–
518). Her words serve to recall Guinevere's remarks about
Arthur:

> *to me*
> *He is all fault who hath no fault at all.*
> *For who loves me must have a touch of earth;*
> *The low sun makes the color. . . .* [*The King is*]
> *A moral child without the craft to rule,*
> *Else had he not lost me.*
>
> ("Lancelot and Elaine," ll. 131–134, 145–146)

Each looks upon love as an escape—Guinevere from almost absolute goodness, Isolt from almost absolute evil. To neither is love a valid emotion nor is the beloved anything more than a means of escape. Guinevere does not wholeheartedly and selflessly love Lancelot any more than Isolt loves Tristram: they love love, not the person. For love is to them an all-consuming emotion which lifts them above an uncongenial reality. Isolt, far more plainly because her passion is far less restrained than Guinevere's, makes this quite evident:

> *the measure of my hate for Mark*
> *Is as the measure of my love for thee!*
>
> (ll. 535–536)

and again:

> *O, were I not my Mark's, by whom all men*
> *Are noble, I should hate thee more than love.*
>
> (ll. 594–595)

The point that Tennyson wishes to make is that in erotic love the lover does not see the beloved; he sees only an object to be possessed. Tristram, for example, can fall in love with a name, the symbol of the object: he marries Isolt of Brittany because of her name: "Did I love her?" he asks of Isolt of the White Hands, "the name at least I loved. . . . The name was ruler of the dark" (ll. 588, 601). In fact, the lovers cannot see because they prefer the dark. The sun, symbol of life itself, is hateful to them. In telling why she does not love Arthur, Guinevere says: "But who can gaze upon the sun in heaven" ("Lancelot and Elaine," l. 123). And the whole love episode of "The Last Tournament" takes place in "the light's last glimmer" (l. 733).

The light imagery of the *Idylls,* as was pointed out in the fourth chapter, should not be overlooked. Arthur comes to slay the beast and fell the forest to let in the sun ("The Coming of Arthur," ll. 59–60), yet nearly all forces militate against his action. The beasts—Vivien and Mark and Modred, all of whom are spoken of in bestial terms—rise up again, and the dark powers, symbolized by the desires of the lovers, work to eclipse the sun. The message is clear: man for the most part does not want life and love, both of which demand active participation, but instead wishes for death, a passive resolution of desire.

Because erotic love seeks to negate life, it is a kind of insanity. The lover will not accept reality; he demands illusion. Isolt asks only to "suck / Lies like sweet wines" and begs Tristram, "Lie to me; I believe" (ll. 639–640). Tristram and Isolt do not love each other; in fact, they all but say they don't. All they need is a passionate dream, some object to substantiate their illusions. Their need of each other is to burn with desire, to escape from a hateful reality. It is an appetite, whetted in Isolt's case as in Guinevere's by jealousy, that is no sooner abated than it rises up again, an appetite that can be satisfied only in death. Tristram makes this evident when, after Isolt's plea for him to lie to her, he says:

> *Come, I am hunger'd and half-anger'd—meat,*
> *Wine, wine—and I will love thee to the death,*
> *And out beyond into the dream to come.*

(ll. 713–715)

The whole scene between Tristram and Isolt is an analysis of how two lovers exploit each other's emotions.

Eros has become deified, and the god has proclaimed oblivion to all else. Tristram tells Isolt: "therefore is my love so large for thee, / Seeing it is not bounded save by love" (ll. 698–699). We are reminded here of Arthur's advice to Lancelot when the knight had said, "free love will not be bound." The King replied, "Free love, so bound, were freest" ("Lancelot and Elaine," ll. 1368–1369). This echo in "The Last Tournament" gives Arthur's words new significance, for we are shown the nature of a love which recognizes only the divinity of passion—this against a background of Tristram's reasons for no longer recognizing the authority of the King. Tennyson brings forward the meaning of these two views of love in Tristram's song:

> *Ay, ay, O, ay, the winds that bend the brier!*
> *A star in heaven, a star within the mere!*
> *Ay, ay, O, ay—a star was my desire,*
> *And one was far apart and one was near.*
> *Ay, ay, O, ay—the winds that bow the grass!*
> *And one was water and one star was fire,*
> *And one will ever shine and one will pass.*
> *Ay, ay, O, ay—the winds that move the mere!*

(ll. 725–732)

Desire is death, as Shakespeare said, and so "Behind him rose a shadow and a shriek— / 'Mark's way,' said Mark, and clove him thro' the brain" (ll. 747–748). The red of the rubies, as was foretold in the dream, becomes the blood of death.

It should be noted that Tennyson omits any mention of the love philtre in the retelling of this famous story. He wants to make perfectly clear that each lover is brought, by an exercise of his own will, to the madness of erotic love. They have the opportunity to choose, and they choose the way which is the opposite to the King's way; nevertheless, the choice is theirs. The justification of the choice is that it is natural: "For feel this arm of mine," says Tristram,

> the tide within
> Red with free chase and heather-scented air,
> Pulsing full man. Can Arthur make me pure
> As any maiden child? lock up my tongue
> From uttering freely what I freely hear?
> Bind me to one? The wide world laughs at it.
> And worlding of the world am I, and know
> The ptarmigan that whitens ere his hour
> Woos his own end; we are not angels here
> Nor shall be. Vows—I am woodman of the woods,
> And hear the garnet-headed yaffingale
> Mock them—my soul, we love but while we may.
>
> (ll. 685–696)

To such a rationalization Arthur would reply that nature provides no justification of conduct. Man is born into "this dark land," a fallen world, which ever stands in need of re-demption, and only through moral development, following an ideal, can man "Have power on this dark land to lighten it, / And power on this dead world to make it live" ("The Coming of Arthur," ll. 92–93). To follow nature, as Tristram argues, is to be swallowed up in darkness.

The linking of love and death is examined on another level of passion in "Lancelot and Elaine," a study of, to use the popular term, "falling in love." Let us note immediately that Elaine falls in love with Lancelot before she even sees him, apparently falling in love with his voice: "the lily maid Elaine, / Won by the mellow voice before she look'd . . . , lifted up her eyes / And loved him, with that love which was her doom" (ll. 241–242, 258–259). In other words, Elaine seems to be in love with love—and as the popular song puts it, "falling in love with love is falling for make-believe." Tennyson shows that this highly praised action is what Ortega has called it: a form of transitory imbecility involving a paralysis of consciousness and a reduction of the habitual world.[4] In such a state the lover so anesthetizes his attention and his will that he is unable to see other than the beloved and, further, unable to see the object of his affection for what in actuality he really is. Elaine deludes herself that Lancelot's every tenderness, every smile is for her: "and she thought / That all was nature, all, perchance, for her" (ll. 327–328). The rest of "Lancelot and Elaine" shows the decline of the maiden who allowed her love to become a mania "and so lived in fantasy" (l. 396).

The lily maid's sad story is that she gives up all sense of her identity to Lancelot—imposes it on him, as it were. Her

[4] *On Love,* p. 51.

passion is but a self-created mask thrown over the lover, and consequently her identity can only be confirmed by her beloved. Thus when she hears from Gawain that Lancelot has been wounded she feels the wound in her own side (ll. 618–621). Without Lancelot she cannot live—" 'Him or death,' she mutter'd, 'death or him' " (l. 897). Passion has so corrupted the will that her wish is to die if she cannot have the man whom she deludes herself she loves: "Being so very wilful you must die," a voice echoes in her ears (l. 778). But death is not a punishment, rather a fulfillment. She penetrates to this perception when she asks Lancelot to allow her to follow him: "I have gone mad. I love you; let me die" (l. 925). Her love is an insanity because it pursues a symbol and not a reality: Elaine has her dream and the dream must be fulfilled.

To her, love and death are inextricably intertwined, for her will is to merge herself with the symbol of her identity and vanish into nothingness. Thus the emotional consummation of her love comes when Lancelot is not even present, and this leads to her song of love and death. "Death, like a friend's voice from a distant field," (l. 992) lures her on, and in her *liebestod* she sings:

> *Sweet is true love tho' given in vain, in vain;*
> *And sweet is death who puts an end to pain.*
> *I know not which is sweeter, no, not I.*
>
> *Love, art thou sweet? then bitter death must be.*
> *Love, thou art bitter; sweet is death to me.*
> *O Love, if death be sweeter, let me die.*

Sweet love, that seems not made to fade away;
Sweet death, that seems to make us loveless clay;
I know not which is sweeter, no, not I.

I fain would follow love, if that could be;
I needs must follow death, who calls for me;
Call and I follow, I follow! let me die.

(ll. 1000–1011)

Her glory, she tells in the final moments of her delusion, is "to have loved / One peerless, without stain" (ll. 1083–1084).

So alarmingly did Tennyson apparently view the insidious qualities of the cult of love that he undertook in "Pelleas and Ettarre" to tell Elaine's story again, this time with a male as the deluded lover. From the beginning of the idyll we see how subject to delusion Pelleas is. While he lies on the ground under a tree to rest on his journey to Camelot, he fancies "that the fern without / Burnt as a living fire of emeralds, / So that his eyes were dazzled looking at it" (ll. 33–35). The trouble with Pelleas evidently is that he is in love with love:

And since he loved all maidens, but no maid
In special, half-awake he whisper'd: 'Where?
O, where? I love thee, tho' I know thee not.'

(ll. 39–41)

In such a state of fictitious love Pelleas needn't wait for a particular object, a "maid in special," to excite his erotic streak, because anyone will serve the purpose. He loves love —that is, like Elaine he lives in fantasy—and what he loves is actually no more than a pretext. He simply invents a love affair, which is what happens when Ettarre by chance comes along.

To him, as to Elaine, it is a case of love at first sight, the object being conceived by his impassioned fantasy. The poet leaves us with no doubt here, as is not entirely the case in "Lancelot and Elaine," that the object of his passion is not worthy of love. As in a dream Pelleas sees—"Strange as to some old prophet might have seem'd / A vision hovering on a sea of fire" (ll. 49–50)—a group of damsels-errant who are on their way to tilt against the knights at Caerleon. He is immediately struck by the beauty of their leader, and there on the spot, at that very moment, he falls uncontrollably in love with Ettarre. That this emotion is nothing more than an exercise in make-believe, a projection onto the object of the values which he wants to find, is indicated by this state-ment on the part of the poet:

> But while he gazed
> The beauty of her flesh abash'd the boy,
> As tho' it were the beauty of her soul;
> For as the base man, judging of the good,
> Puts his own baseness in him by default
> Of will and nature, so did Pelleas lend
> All the young beauty of his own soul to hers. . . .

(ll. 73–79)

Ettarre openly makes fun of him, yet, so enthralled by his delusion, Pelleas believes that her and her maidens' laugh-ing at him is simply a sign of joy. "O happy world," he thinks, "all, meseems, / Are happy" (ll. 129–130). As the nar-rator tells us, "he dream'd / His lady loved him" (ll. 145–146).

Poor Pelleas completely resigns his will to hers. Although a knight of Arthur's, he is "More bondsman in his heart than in his bonds" and becomes the vassal of her will (ll. 231–233), allowing her wishes to take precedence over the King's. Will-less and rapt in fantasy, Pelleas time after time refuses to recognize things for what they are. When Ettarre is rude and cruel to him, he deludes himself that these be the ways of ladies to test those that love them. By overwhelming the object of his love with attention and concentration, his consciousness endows it with a force of reality. It becomes more real than anything else. Again through song Tennyson lets us see clearly the nature of erotic love:

> *One rose, my rose, that sweeten'd all mine air—*
> *I cared not for the thorns; the thorns were there.*
>
> *One rose, a rose to gather by and by,*
> *One rose, a rose, to gather and to wear,*
> *No rose but one—what other rose had I?*
> *One rose, my rose; a rose that will not die,—*
> *He dies who loves it,—if the worm be there.*
>
> (ll. 394–400)

It means oblivion to reality, and death.

Unlike Elaine, Pelleas awakens from his romantic dream, an awakening which comes when he finds Gawain and Ettarre lying together. Only at the moment of this psychic shock is the maniac's haven broken down and channels of sealed consciousness opened to sobering fresh air. Pelleas is then allowed the perception that "I never loved her, I but lusted for her" (l. 475). And so love dies because its inception was an error. Yet Pelleas is unable or unwilling to act on his new consciousness. For, like Elaine, if he can't find reality measuring up to his preconceptions, his dreams of how the world should be, then he will have nothing to do with it at all. He therefore blames the King for his insane actions and rushes off like a beast to become Arthur's antagonist. Eros deified has become demonic. Always we are returned to the author's central point: love without cosmological inspiration ends in defeat, sterility, and death.

The other love affairs in the *Idylls* serve as preparation for the four which I have just discussed. Gareth attempts to win Lynette's respect by doing the King's work, and he succeeds. The idyll is not, however, primarily a love story, for we are never allowed to see Gareth winning the maiden for his own. The narrator closes the episode by saying:

> *And he that told the tale in olden times*
> *Says that Sir Gareth wedded Lyonors,*
> *But he that told it later says Lynette.*

The two idylls concerned with Geraint and Enid, on the other hand, are designed to show that something is wrong in Camelot and that Geraint's treatment of Enid is symptomatic of this evil. The rumor of disloyalty on the part of Guinevere and Lancelot is enough to stir in Geraint doubts about the validity of his vows to the King; and questioning the King, the one to whom he has sworn everlasting faith, he begins to question everything else, even his wife Enid.

Enid has never given her husband any cause for doubting

her faithfulness, yet suspicious of her he takes her away from the court to his princedom. Here

> *He compass'd her with sweet observances*
> *And worship, never leaving her, and grew*
> *Forgetful of his promise to the King. . . ,*
> *Forgetful of his glory and his name,*
> *Forgetful of his princedom and its cares.*
>
> ("The Marriage of Geraint," ll. 48–50, 53–54)

To calm his anguish of jealousy, which is announced here for the first time in the *Idylls* and is thematically developed in the Lancelot-Guinevere and Tristram-Isolt episodes, Geraint wishes his wife to be constantly before his eyes, to hold her in thrall just as Proust's Marcel desires to hold Albertine captive. In retreating to this kind of vegetable existence Geraint forswears the vows of service made to Arthur. In time, however, Enid proves herself, and his old affections return when he rids himself of all notions of romantic love and returns to his duty.

The conflict between service and passion is presented allegorically in "Merlin and Vivien." Merlin seems to sum up within himself Western civilization's whole cultural accomplishment: he "knew the range of all their arts, / Had built the King his havens, ships, and halls, / Was also bard, and knew the starry heavens" (ll. 165–167). Vivien, on the other hand, is representative of all those forces which seek to deny man's moral and cultural development and whose source is death. She is indeed a child of death: "for born from death was I / Among the dead and sown upon the wind" (ll. 44–45). Her greatest wish is to inactivate the qualities which Merlin represents, and she knows that her only means of achieving this lies in the charm which Merlin possesses and which she must in some way wrest from his control.

The charm is apparently erotic passion, the willingness to surrender the will to desire. The secret of the charm had originated with an old wizard, a hermit who by denying desire had seen into the nature of the human condition. The seer had taught the charm to an ancient king who, stimulated by misguided passion, wished to conquer wholly his stolen bride and "Keep her all his own." Knowing the secret the king wrought its effect upon his queen, who then "lay as dead, / And lost all use of life" (ll. 642–643). Enchanted by the prospect of using this weapon on Merlin, Vivien employs all her wiles to obtain the secret.

In his most perspicacious moments Merlin realizes that Vivien's wheedling is a "vice in you which ruin'd man / Thro' woman the first hour" (ll. 360–361). For a man to surrender himself utterly to a woman means the surrender of one's will to Eros, which involves the loss of self not only to the world but also to God. A teleological suspension of the ethical, Tennyson makes quite plain, is valid only in the case of a man like Galahad, who in losing himself by sitting in the Siege Perilous had found himself in giving himself to God. Yet for most men, even for the best like Merlin, the ethical is enjoined upon them and cannot be suspended except to their peril. This is why the Siege Perilous is perilous for good and ill, why Merlin is lost when he sits in it ("The Holy Grail," ll. 166–178). For as Yeats said in "Ego Dominus Tuus," those that love the world serve it in action, those that deny the claims of action have as their portion dissipation and despair.

Vivien's wiles are those characteristic of the romantic lover. She argues that the only worthy love is that which seeks only itself to please. Love is, she says, an escape from time, a transcendence of the temporal whereby time is re-deemed; it "carves / A portion from the present, eats / And uses, careless of the rest" (ll. 459–461). It is a giving up of one's self heedlessly, a union of selves which involves loss of individual identity: "My name, once mine, now thine, is closelier mine, / For fame, could fame be mine, that fame were thine, / And shame, could shame be thine, that shame were mine" (ll. 444–446). Merlin, however, pleads that love must yield to service:

> *Love*
> *Should have some rest and pleasure in himself,*
> *Not ever be too curious for a boon,*
> *Too prurient for a proof against the grain*
> *Of him ye say ye love. But Fame with men,*
> *Being but ampler means to serve mankind,*
> *Should have small rest or pleasure in herself,*
> *But work as vassal to the larger love*
> *That dwarfs the petty love of one to one.*

(ll. 482–490)

Merlin argues this rationally, yet in the end he is unable to withstand Vivien's temptations. Merlin had worked in the King's service to procure for Arthur, the ideal man, accept-ance, authority, and power; but by the late summer of the

King's reign the wizard sees, as I have attempted to demonstrate in earlier chapters, that the principle from which so much good was hoped has seemed to fail of its goal. He is disheartened by the way things are going in Camelot and he falls into despair:

> *Then fell on Merlin a great melancholy;*
> *He walk'd with dreams and darkness, and he found*
> *A doom that ever poised itself to fall,*
> *An ever-moaning battle in the mist,*
> *World-war of dying flesh against the life,*
> *Death in all life and lying in all love,*
> *The meanest having power upon the highest,*
> *And the high purpose broken by the worm.*
>
> (ll. 187–194)

Merlin's position, the poet suggests, is that of the man of intellect in the modern world. The reason sees the antinomy between principle and result, and, because the result is not what logically should have followed, the reason begins to doubt the validity of the principle. It begins to put its trust in other things. So at the beginning of the idyll we find Merlin escaping from Camelot—running off to the woods just as Balin and Tristram do, retreating to the darkness of the forest which Arthur felled to let in the light—and in Broceliande, with Vivien, the fiend of darkness, at his side, hoping to find some ease for his melancholy: "at times / Would flatter his own wish in age for love, / And half believe her true" (ll. 182–184).

Tennyson does not allow us to forget the real nature of Vivien. When she follows Merlin abroad, the poet tells us that "as an enemy that has left / Death in the living waters and withdrawn, / The wily Vivien stole from Arthur's court" (ll. 145–147). Further we are told how when she is angered with the wizard her terrible nature stands revealed: "How from the rosy lips of life and love / Flash'd the bare-grinning skeleton of death!" (ll. 844–845). Yet Merlin refuses to act on what he sees; so obsessed is the intellect with the presumed failure of what once was a guiding principle that in its desire for refuge from its despair it turns to what is immediately at hand. Merlin turns to Vivien, hoping by indulging the senses to assuage the pangs of the heart and mind: he "let his wisdom go / For ease of heart" (ll. 890–891). He tells her the secret of the charm, which serves the same function as the love potion in the myth of Tristram and Isolt, and she enchants him: "he lay as dead, / Lost to life and use and name and fame." By submitting to passion he becomes as dead to the world. The reason no longer controls passion but is enslaved by it. The submission of reason to passion brings the end which Shakespeare wrote of in sonnet 147: "Past cure I am, now reason is past care, / And frantic-mad with evermore unrest." Thus does "Merlin and Vivien" establish the pattern to be followed in the succeeding idylls. Desire is death, and Lancelot, Tristram, and Merlin are destroyed by those agents of death, all so characterized—Modred, Mark, and Vivien.

With the possible exception of Wagner no one in the nineteenth century, I believe, explored so thoroughly or so well as Tennyson the psychology of erotic love. To believe in redemption by love is, he says, to believe in a chimera, since the essence of passion is illusion. Erotic love is, Tennyson showed, a projection of the self onto an object in an attempt to confirm the identity of the self by recognizing it in the object. This of course means that the object is violated when it is regarded as an instrument. The lover exploits the beloved, but at the same time he becomes dependent on the beloved to prove himself to himself. Thus in erotic love the lover sees only himself in his beloved, and thus is passion a form of narcissism. Necessarily, then, passion consumes that by which it was nourished. In the end the lover is left only with desire for utter possession, a desire that cannot be fulfilled in life; the goal of love thereupon becomes death, a fading away into nothingness.

True love, on the other hand, is not motivated by the illusory nature of passion. To be sure, passion is part of love—and Tennyson never seeks to deny this; but love transcends passion because its goal is not absolute possession. True love is a striving for perfection—perfection not only of self but of the world. It consequently never becomes an end in itself because it is predicated on something other than itself. Eros, in other words, is redeemed by Agape, which is the earthly expression of the great cosmological principle; this point Tennyson had proved to his own satisfaction in *In Memoriam,* where love of Hallam the Christlike man had redeemed the "I" from dependence on Hallam the object of a purely personal emotion. One loves, says Tennyson, only when Love, not love, is his lord and king, or as stated in the Prologue to *In Memoriam,* "Our wills are ours, to make them Thine."

In the *Idylls of the King* Arthur is the earthly representative of the divine principle of charity. Trust in him, "In whom high God hath breathed a secret thing" ("The Coming of Arthur," l. 500), provides the cosmological inspiration necessary for love. Galahad alone may legitimately deny the authority of the King over himself but only because Galahad had communed with Love Itself. All others in Camelot, however, can love only when they trust in the King, the intermediator between Love and love. To turn to love without the authority of Love is to submit to the abnegation of love—death.

❖ VI

"The Holy Grail": Vision vs. duty

Tennyson's interest in mystical experience is well known. In a number of works prior to the *Idylls* the resolution to the problem set forth issues from the protagonist's retreat into an irrational state which provides profounder insights than waking consciousness. The climaxes to *In Memoriam*, for example, occur when the "I" communes with the dead friend in trance (in Lyric XCV) and dream (in Lyric CIII). Tennyson himself said:

> A kind of waking trance I have frequently had, quite up from boyhood, when I have been all alone. This has generally come upon me thro' repeating my own name two or three times to myself silently, till all at once, as it were out of the intensity of the consciousness of individuality, the individuality itself seemed to dissolve and fade away into boundless being, and this not a confused state, but the clearest of the clearest, the surest of the surest, the weirdest of the weirdest, utterly beyond words, where death was an almost laughable impossibility, the loss of personality (if so it were) seeming no extinction but the only true life.
>
> (*Memoir*, I, 320)

Yet for all his interest in irrational states of mind Tennyson focused his vision on the present here and now. With the existentialist he would agree that to know truth as an abstraction is pointless; what matters is how it affects man's life. Hence we find in Tennyson's poetry a philosophy of action with an insistence on self-committal.

It is not surprising, therefore, that the poet consistently condemns the ascetic who, scorning the duties of the ethical life, withdraws into isolation and becomes contemptuous of the world. In "St. Simeon Stylites" Tennyson attacks, by letting the speaker expose himself, the anchorite's religious asceticism, which manifests itself in masochism and spiritual perversion. Similarly, in the *Idylls of the King,* in "Balin and Balan," the first idyll to have a tragic ending, Tennyson again shows the malevolent results of religious fanaticism. King Pellam evades his kingly duties by retreating into a sacerdotal life and refusing to accept responsibility, stating, "I have quite foregone / All matters of this world" (ll. 113–114). He has taken to holy matters and traced his lineage back to Joseph of Arimathea; furthermore, he keeps a shrine where are contained

> *Rich arks with priceless bones of martyrdom,*
> *Thorns of the crown and shivers of the cross,*
> *And therewithal,—for thus he told us,—brought*
> *By holy Joseph hither, that same spear*
> *Wherewith the Roman pierced the side of Christ.*
>
> (ll. 107–111)

It should be noted that it is in this context that mention of Joseph of Arimathea and his relics first appears. These holy things are placed in a gloomy castle situated in a murky wood where wanderers become lost and confused, where twin brothers mistake each other for fiends, where is situated what may be the mouth of hell. Moreover, this forest is inhabited by a monster which attacks people from behind; yet Pellam does nothing to rid his environs of this evil, so engrossed is he in religious ceremony. Finally, it should be noted that the sacred spear brought by Joseph of Arimathea is the instrument by which one brother slays another.

In "Merlin and Vivien" the theme of asceticism is again introduced. A wandering minstrel visits Mark's court and tells how, although Arthur has not bound them to celibacy, some of the knights of the Round Table are "So passionate for an utter purity / Beyond the limit of their bond" (ll. 26–27). When Mark and Vivien hear that certain knights have exceeded in asceticism their vows to the King, they realize that here lies an opening at Camelot through which they can destroy Arthur's kingdom.

In this manner Tennyson prepares his reader for "The Holy Grail," wherein the Cup becomes a symbol of social disintegration. This was indeed a daring departure. One might well ask why the poet undertook a rendering of the Grail legend when, because of personal inclination, he would be forced to deal with it in such an unorthodox way. The answer is, first, that he had been contemplating a poem on the subject for many years, "ever since he began to write about Arthur and his knights" (*Memoir*, II, 65), and, secondly, that some of his most influential readers wanted an idyll based on the Grail theme. Not only Macaulay, the

Duke of Argyll, and Mrs. Tennyson, but also the Crown Princess and the Queen herself wanted that the "High History of the Holy Grail should form a part of the Idylls." Yet the idea of an idyll devoted to the Grail presented the Laureate with many problems. As he wrote in 1859, "I doubt whether such a subject could be handled in these days without incurring a charge of irreverence. It would be too much like playing with sacred things. The old writers *believed* in the Sangreal" (*Memoir,* I, 456–457).

For at least ten years Tennyson brooded over the problem of how the Grail theme should be treated. When the solution was found, the poet sat down and wrote rapidly. "He had never written with more intense inspiration," his biographer grandson tells us, "nor had his family ever seen his face more continually bear the rapt expression which showed complete absorption in his subject." [1]

The question which now presents itself is this: What *was* Tennyson's solution? The answer is that the poet decided to depart from his practice in the other idylls, which are told from the point of view of an omniscient narrator, and make "The Holy Grail" a first-person narrative. But, we ask, how is this a solution? In the first place, the use of Percivale as narrator could serve as a safety device: if questioned he could reply, in the manner of Browning, these are the views of a fictitious person, not mine. Secondly, in using Percivale as narrator Tennyson could involve his audience in the story and have them accept it uncritically by calling on the special merits of the dramatic monologue. I realize, of course, that

[1] Charles Tennyson, *Alfred Tennyson* (London, 1949), p. 378.

technically "The Holy Grail" is not a dramatic monologue but specifically a dialogue between Percivale and Ambrosius. I believe, however, that Tennyson first conceived of Ambrosius, if indeed he was part of the poet's original conception of this idyll, as merely a listener (I shall discuss this point later in this chapter), included only to provide a dramatic situation in which Percivale could express himself.

Mr. Robert Langbaum has spoken of the dramatic monologue as a poetry of sympathy, its "end being to establish the reader's sympathetic relation to the poem, to give him 'facts from within.' " [2] In such a poem the reader identifies himself with the speaker and so suspends moral judgment of him, which is, Mr. Langbaum says, the price we pay for the privilege of appreciating the speaker to the full. There is thus a tension in the dramatic monologue between sympathy and moral judgment. The reader sees events and other characters through the speaker's eyes, and it is, consequently, the speaker who determines the significance of the parts and, finally, the meaning of the poem.

Tennyson had, of course, learned years before the value of the dramatic monologue: in the same year that Browning published his first experiments in the form, Tennyson had, with "Ulysses" and "St. Simeon Stylites," used the dramatic monologue with perfect skill. But from 1842 to the late sixties he had neglected the form, unless we accept "Maud" as a poem of this genre. Then in 1868 he wrote "Lucretius," a poem in which he sought to show how, as Sir Charles Ten-

[2] Robert Langbaum, *The Poetry of Experience* (New York, 1957), p. 78.

nyson says, "a theme of the kind could be handled seriously without offence" (p. 375). The means he chose for such an attempt was, of course, the dramatic monologue; and the success of "Lucretius" determined, I feel it highly likely, the solution to the Grail idyll.

I think it important to bear in mind Mr. Langbaum's observations because in "The Holy Grail" we see everything that happens through the eyes of Percivale. Identifying ourselves uncritically with him, we have to accept his version of the Grail story and his version of the knights' experiences because we have no other. It is he, and not the omniscient narrator, who determines the meaning of the narrative. For we not only accept his version of the story but also accept his conception of himself. Our sympathy and identification with him even cause us to accept his idea of the King; with him we believe, for the moment at least, that "the King was hard upon his knights" (l. 299), and we share his puzzlement at Arthur's closing words: "So spake the King; I knew not all he meant." All this means that our immediate understanding of "The Holy Grail" is one of sympathy with a pure knight who, despite the opposition of his king and all manner of spiritual and physical obstacles, perseveres in his quest for the Holy Cup until he has his vision of it and then, having seen, retires to "the silent life of prayer." This, I say, is our *first* response to the poem, just as our first understanding of St. Simeon is of a holy anchorite; in other words, caught up in the dramatic utterance, we suspend our moral judgment of the speaker.

"The Holy Grail" is not, however, so simple a poem that

it communicates only on one level of meaning. For when we reread the idyll and reflect on it in context, we see that we cannot accept without reservation everything that Percivale says; we see, in fact, that even Percivale's conception of himself leaves something else to be said.

The first mention of Percivale occurs in "Merlin and Vivien," when Vivien, at her malicious worst, accusing Arthur's knights of the most sordid crimes, assails the character of Percivale; but he is defended by Merlin, who says: "And that he sinn'd is not believable" (l. 758). He next is mentioned in "Lancelot and Elaine," when "Arthur bade the meek Sir Percivale / And pure Sir Galahad" to carry the dead Elaine from the barge into the hall (ll. 1256–1257). These two references are certainly to Percivale's credit, although we must remember that they were written in the later 1850's, more than a decade before Tennyson undertook the writing of "The Holy Grail." The only other mention of Percivale comes in "Pelleas and Ettarre," an idyll written *after* "The Holy Grail." Upon waking from a dream, Pelleas,

> *being ware of some one nigh,*
> *Sent hands upon him, as to tear him, crying,*
> *'False! and I held thee pure as Guinevere.'*

> *But Percivale stood near him and replied,*
> *'Am I but false as Guinevere is pure?*
> *Or art thou mazed with dreams? or being one*
> *Of our free-spoken Table hast not heard*
> *That Lancelot'—there he check'd himself and paused.*

> *Then fared it with Sir Pelleas as with one*
> *Who gets a wound in battle, and the sword*
> *That made it plunges thro' the wound again,*
> *And pricks it deeper; and he shrank and wail'd,*
> *'Is the Queen false?' and Percivale was mute.*
> *'Have any of our Round Table held their vows?'*
> *And Percivale made answer not a word.*
> *'Is the King true?' 'The King!' said Percivale.*
> *'Why, then let men couple at once with wolves.*
> *What! art thou mad?'*

(ll. 509–527)

The picture of Percivale here is that of a scandalmonger. Maybe this is too harsh a judgment upon the knight, but at any rate the incident is not entirely to Percivale's credit. Tennyson could have used almost any other character in the *Idylls* for this episode, but I am inclined to believe that he chose Percivale because, "Pelleas and Ettarre" having been written later than "The Holy Grail," he had a clear idea of what Percivale was like.

In the idyll under consideration Percivale is not, if we look closely, a character entirely to be admired. First let us recall that Percivale is not credited with one glorious deed or unselfish act in any of the idylls. Neither in fearsome exploit nor in brave act in tournament does he bring the "glory" which the King rejoices in. "No keener hunter after glory breathes," says Guinevere of Arthur. "He loves it in his knights more than himself" ("Lancelot and Elaine," ll. 155–156). Percivale, on the other hand, regards the King's tournaments as events which "waste the spiritual strength / Within us, better offer'd up to heaven" (ll. 35–36). Yet he is eager to talk about the tournament in which he did excel, the last tournament before the quest, and is not at all modest about the number of knights he overthrew or the praise he received from the people.

As a knight of the Round Table Percivale is, I think we are clearly given to understand, something of a failure. Having failed to distinguish himself in knightly "glory," he eagerly turns to the Grail quest when the idea presents itself. By the time of "The Holy Grail" something is clearly wrong in Camelot; and Percivale, I believe, epitomizes the unrest in Arthur's kingdom. The ideal of service, the "use" which Merlin speaks of and loses, has almost disappeared: self-fulfillment, not selfless duty, becomes the goal among the knights; and the alacrity with which they jump at the chance to seek the Grail suggests this change which the state has undergone.

Percivale is the first of the knights to hear the story of the reappearance of the Grail; and no sooner does he hear than he dashes off to court to tell the news:

> *I spake of this*
> *To all the men; and myself fasted and pray'd*
> *Always, and many among us many a week*
> *Fasted and pray'd even to the uttermost,*
> *Expectant of the wonder that would be.*

(ll. 129–133)

The impression we get here is of a group of men who, disaffected with their present life, are out for a new sensation, who, suffering spiritual *ennui*, are ready to *"plonger au fond de l'Inconnu pour trouver du nouveau."* In other words, Arthur's knights are like those men of the last half of the nineteenth century who in reaction to their spiritual malaise sought so passionately for the *frissons nouveaux* offered by Madame Blavatsky.

Not only is Percivale the first to inform the court of this new interest, he is also the first to swear that he will ride in quest of it. If outshone in "glory," he will not be outdone in spiritual enthusiasm:

> *all the knights arose,*
> *And staring each at other like dumb men*
> *Stood, till I found a voice and sware a vow.*
>
> *I sware a vow before them all, that I,*
> *Because I had not seen the Grail, would ride*
> *A twelvemonth and a day in quest of it,*
> *Until I found and saw it, as the nun*
> *My sister saw it; and Galahad sware the vow,*
> *And good Sir Bors, our Lancelot's cousin, sware,*
> *And Lancelot sware, and many among the knights,*
> *And Gawain sware, and louder than the rest.*
>
> (ll. 192–202)

As Arthur says, "one hath seen, and all the blind will see" (l. 313). None of the knights will be outdone by any of the rest; even Gawain, the least spiritual of Arthur's knights, swears, "and louder than the rest."

It is important at this point to recall once again the knights' vows to the King. In "The Coming of Arthur" they had sworn to "work thy will," they were "Bound by so straight vows *to his own self*" (italics mine); in spiritual matters they were to seek enlightenment through him:

The King will follow Christ, and we the King,
In whom high God hath breathed a secret thing.

He for God, they for God in him. Yet here they are abrogating their vows to the King, in direct contradiction to what they had previously sworn. No wonder then that Arthur is wroth when he returns and finds out what has transpired.

As a result of the experience undergone Percivale feels himself immeasurably elevated in the ranks of Camelot. In reply to the King's question about what has happened, he addresses Arthur, *the King,* as "O brother," certainly a classic example of *lèse majesté*. And in the ensuing account of the King's reaction to their new vow Percivale makes a point of the fact that he is held among the most spiritual of the knights at Camelot (ll. 306–308). And for all the commotion, it turns out that neither Percivale, nor for that matter any of the knights in the hall save Galahad, has actually seen the Grail; so thrilled by the electrifying experience described in lines 182–190, he has sworn his vow simply because he did not see:

> *But since I did not see the holy thing,*
> *I sware a vow to follow it till I saw.*
>
> (ll. 281–282)

And the other knights, following Percivale's example, answer likewise.

Upon analysis, then, the picture that emerges of Percivale is of a vain, self-centered, irresponsible knight. Percivale is guilty of the sin of pride. One has only to compare him with

Bors to see how truly deficient he is in humility. Imagine if possible Percivale speaking like this:

> '*And then to me, to me,'*
> *Said good Sir Bors, 'beyond all hopes of mine,*
> *Who scarce had pray'd or ask'd it for myself . . .*
>   *the sweet Grail*
> *Glided and past. . . .'*

(ll. 686–692)

Here, in Sir Bors's account, marked by the natural humility of the good knight, lies a striking contrast to the tone of nearly all Percivale's recountings of his experiences. Sir Bors would gladly have foregone his glimpse of the Grail so that his cousin Lancelot might have seen. It is unthinkable that Percivale would have given up his sight of the Cup for anyone.

Moreover, not only pride but also a certain obtuseness, which is perhaps the blindness that accompanies pride, characterizes Percivale. Consider, for example, his account of the knights' departure for the quest:

>   *where the roofs*
> *Totter'd toward each other in the sky,*
> *Met foreheads all along the street of those*
> *Who watch'd us pass; and lower, and where the long*
> *Rich galleries, lady-laden, weigh'd the necks*
> *Of dragons clinging to the crazy walls,*
> *Thicker than drops from thunder, showers of flowers*
> *Fell as we past; and men and boys astride*
> *Of wyvern, lion, dragon, griffin, swan,*
> *At all the corners, named us each by name,*
> *Calling 'God speed!' but in the ways below*

> *The knights and ladies wept, and rich and poor*
> *Wept, and the King himself could hardly speak*
> *For grief.*

(ll. 342–355)

Percivale obviously has no understanding of this scene. The plaudits of the crowd he revels in; the weeping he does not comprehend. Percivale is the camera which records but cannot interpret. The degree of his responsiveness to the mournful parting is revealed in the ensuing lines:

> *And I was lifted up in heart, and thought*
> *Of all my late-shown prowess in the lists,*
> *How my strong lance had beaten down the knights,*
> *So many and famous names.*

(ll. 361–364)

Finally, there is in Percivale more than a little of the desire to escape reality and so evade responsibility. In a preceding chapter I have suggested the degree of emotional dependency in Percivale and others of Arthur's Order, and I should like here to suggest further that the strict vow enjoined on Percivale by the King has resulted in the knight's realization of his inability to live up to what is expected of him, causing most probably the defensive vanity which he so frequently manifests. The quest offers the chance to retreat into a phantasmal dream world. When the bridges behind Galahad spring into fire and vanish, Percivale reports, "I yearn'd / To follow" (ll. 506–507). And even after his glimpse of the Grail in the distance he is not satisfied to return to his duties at Camelot. Unable to pass with Galahad into the world beyond, he chooses the next best

situation by withdrawing to a monastery. Pure and meek
though he is considered by the other knights at Camelot, we
see him in another aspect—and so most likely does Arthur,
who in the simplest words but most derogatory tone says
of him:

> *Another hath beheld it afar off,*
> *And, leaving human wrongs to right themselves,*
> *Cares but to pass into the silent life.*

(ll. 893–895)

If my interpretation of Percivale's character is correct,
why then did Tennyson choose Percivale as the narrator? To
answer this we must consider what the idyll would be like if
it were told from the point of view of the omniscient author.
In the first place, if we were looking down on the episode
from above, the actions of the Grail knights would seem
implausible and perhaps a little ridiculous. In the second
place, had Tennyson chosen this point of view, he would
have been faced with the problem of how to deal with the
religious aspects of the story—indeed a problem for an
author who does not share the religious beliefs, which trigger
the action of the episode, of his characters. In the third
place, the point of view of the omniscient author would
have presented the further problem as to which of the Grail
knights to sympathize with, a solution to which would
necessarily have forced the poet to expose his own views. By
using the first-person narrative, therefore, Tennyson was
able to escape implausibility and the possibility of offending
his readers' religious beliefs.

But why Percivale, why not one of the other knights as narrator? The answer here is that Percivale is sufficiently, but not excessively, flawed to serve as a pole of sympathy. Of the five knights figuring prominently in this idyll Percivale is the only one Tennyson could have employed in this manner. Galahad is the saint, and to render the world from his point of view would have been well-nigh impossible. Furthermore, if we were to see the story through his eyes, where would the story end? Gawain can be eliminated as a candidate for precisely the opposite reasons: he never got far on the quest and so saw nothing, being, as Arthur says, "too blind to have desire to see" (1. 868). Lancelot's former madness returns when he goes in search of the Grail, and this in itself, along with the fact that he did not see the Grail, is enough to preclude him as a possible narrator. As for Bors, he is too little caught up in the quest, too little interested in the search (although because of his unselfishness and disinterestedness he is allowed sight of the Cup) to serve as a sympathetic narrator. Of the five knights, Percivale is morally and spiritually the central figure, as I shall try to show presently. Less spiritual than Galahad and less selfless than Bors but morally superior to Gawain and Lancelot, Percivale stands in the middle. He was the obvious, and only possible, choice for narrator.

Earlier I mentioned that Ambrosius seems to have played only a very minor part in Tennyson's original conception of "The Holy Grail." Sir Charles Tennyson tells us that the description at the beginning of Percivale's friendship with Ambrosius and Ambrosius' interruption starting with line

540 were not present in the first drafts of the poem.[3] One wonders, therefore, why the poet felt it necessary to give the monk a greater role in the idyll; for readers generally have found him tiresome.

The main function he serves is simply that of providing Percivale someone to talk to. Ambrosius is an interlocutor: he asks questions and Percivale replies. But merely as a kind of confidant, he is a very crude narrative device. Evidently, if we grant Tennyson any narrative skill at all, he must have been included for some additional reason. Now, if we examine Ambrosius' utterances, we see that he is not simply a neutral listener but through his questions points up, and in effect comments upon, Percivale's character and the whole episode of the Grail quest.

In the beginning we learn that he is an extremely warm, sympathetic figure who delights in Percivale's friendship in this monastery "Where all the brethren are so hard" (l. 617), which utterance is undoubtedly the author's comment on monastic life. He loves the village people with their homely joys and destinies obscure (ll. 546–560). In a word he is a realist who takes pleasure and finds meaning in the real world, and as such he stands in strongest contrast to Percivale and the other knights who go off in quest of visions and miracles and marvels. Furthermore, he is incredulous. He spends much time in the monastery library, and has learned from books of the coming of Joseph of Arimathea to Glastonbury and has even become familiar with some of the more obscure details of the story, such as the name of the

[3] Charles Tennyson, *Six Tennyson Essays* (London, 1954), pp. 160–161.

prince (Arviragus) who gave Joseph the ground on which to build a church. Yet—and this is most significant, I believe— he has never read or heard of the Grail story. He says this first in lines 65–66 and then repeats it in lines 541–544, the passage which did not exist in Tennyson's first draft. Furthermore, he calls the Grail "The phantom of a cup that comes and goes" (l. 44).

It should be noted here that to Ambrosius it is the Grail which is a phantom. To Percivale, on the other hand, it is people who are phantoms. Seeking always what is now journalistically called "the human-interest angle," Ambrosius asks: "Came ye on none but phantoms in your quest, / No man, no woman?" And Percivale replies: "All men, to one so bound by such a vow, / And women were as phantoms" (ll. 562–565). In the dialogue between Ambrosius and Percivale we find, therefore, the monk employed not only as interlocutor and chorus-figure but also as contrast to Percivale—Ambrosius representing the humanitarian realist and Percivale representing the sensation-seeking visionary.

Of the 916 lines composing "The Holy Grail," only eighty-six are devoted to Ambrosius. He speaks seven times, and each time his utterance is in contrast to, or an implied comment upon, Percivale's views. In the beginning he asks: "Tell me, what drove thee from the Table Round, / My brother? was it earthly passion crost?" (ll. 28–29), which question gives us a pretty good idea of Ambrosius' reality-centered nature. In his second and third questions (ll. 37–44, 59–67) he enunciates his ignorance of the Grail story. His fourth question comes after Percivale's account of the knights' vows to quest for the Grail: it consists of only one line: "What said the King? Did Arthur take the vow?" (l. 204), apparently inserted here to point up the fact that Arthur had no part in this mysterious experience. The fifth time Ambrosius speaks he reiterates his ignorance of the miraculous Grail and suggests, by means of the last two lines, the hallucination which Percivale had been undergoing. Because the passage is an important one, I quote it here at some length:

> '*O brother,' ask'd Ambrosius,—'for in sooth*
> *These ancient books—and they would win thee—teem,*
> *Only I find not there this Holy Grail,*
> *With miracles and marvels like to these,*
> *Not all unlike; which oftentime I read,*
> *Who read but on my breviary with ease,*
> *Till my head swims, and then go forth and pass*
> *Down to the little thorpe that lies so close,*
> *And almost plaster'd like a martin's nest*
> *To these old walls—and mingle with our folk;*
> *And knowing every honest face of theirs*
> *As well as ever shepherd knew his sheep,*
> *And every homely secret in their hearts,*
> *Delight myself with gossip and old wives,*
> *And ills and aches, and teethings, lyings-in,*
> *And mirthful sayings, children of the place,*
> *That have no meaning half a league away;*
> *Or lulling random squabbles when they rise,*
> *Chafferings and chatterings at the market-cross,*
> *Rejoice, small man, in this small world of mine,*
> *Yea, even in their hens and in their eggs—*
> *O brother, saving this Sir Galahad,*
> *Came ye on none but phantoms in your quest,*
> *No man, no woman?'*

(ll. 540–563)

What is most striking about this passage is the context in which it occurs. It comes immediately after Percivale's long narrative of his quest, and thus it stands in stunning contrast to Percivale's whole religious and moral outlook.

Ambrosius' next interruption goes far to explain what seems to be an irrelevant, at least a somewhat enigmatic, part of Percivale's account of his experiences on the quest. Percivale has been explaining how he meets with the woman he once loved who, now a widowed princess, asks him to marry her and rule over her land; he also tells that the people likewise ask him to become their ruler. Percivale relates that he is strongly tempted to accept her love and to become a useful citizen but that "after I was join'd with Galahad / Cared not for her nor anything upon earth" (ll. 610–611). It has been suggested that this episode "seems better suited for the fantasies of a thrifty Methodist shopkeeper than for the experience of a member of the Table Round." [4] Such a criticism would be pertinent if we were to see Percivale as a wholly sympathetic figure who is momentarily kept from a holy quest by this temptation. But, as I have tried to demonstrate, Percivale reveals himself not as a man of religious vocation who is to be emulated nor is the quest revealed as a wholly worthy endeavor. For in this instance Tennyson uses Ambrosius as the means by which he allows us to know that he thinks the widowed princess episode not exactly a temptation. Ambrosius says:

[4] Donald Smalley, "A New Look At Tennyson—And Especially the *Idylls*," *JEGP*, LXI (1962), 354.

O the pity
To find thine own first love once more—to hold,
Hold her a wealthy bride within thine arms,
Or all but hold, and then—cast her aside,
Foregoing all her sweetness, like a weed!
For we that want the warmth of double life,
We that are plagued with dreams of something sweet
Beyond all sweetness in a life so rich,—

(ll. 618–625)

at which point he breaks off. Here I believe Tennyson is using Ambrosius not only to comment upon the unnatural state of monasticism but also to suggest that in fleeing from the woman he loves Percivale has not necessarily made the right choice.

The last time Ambrosius interrupts is to praise the character of Sir Bors, who attains the vision of the Grail, and to ask whether Arthur's prophecy of the results of the quest was realized (ll. 696–707). The point of the monk's speech here is, I believe, to emphasize the difference between the selfish Percivale and the unselfish Bors. Since I shall treat Bors's character later in this chapter, I shall not at this point discuss further Ambrosius' comment upon him.

From an examination of the seven times he speaks in "The Holy Grail" we see that Ambrosius, in a far more sophisticated manner than the little novice in "Guinevere," serves as a foil—and not only foil but also chorus-figure. Ambrosius is capable of empathy, of love and compassion, in a way that the religious fanatics of his monastery and the self-centered Percivale are not. It is as unthinkable that Ambrosius would go off chasing wandering fires through a quagmire and con-sider such religion as it would be for Arthur. And here we finally arrive at the truth of Ambrosius' function: Ambrosius is Arthur on a smaller scale. An ethically oriented individ-ual, he conceives of religion as an adjunct to the ethical life. As long as man stands in need he sees it as one's duty to help his fellows, and to him any suspension of the ethical obli-gations must attend the day when, as Arthur says, "his work is done" (l. 905). It is significant, I feel, that for the last 208 lines Ambrosius disappears. His place in the idyll is taken by Arthur, who in his final speech reiterates in essence all that Ambrosius had previously implied. And Percivale's final words—"So spake the King; I knew not all he meant."—show the knight as uncomprehending of Arthur and what he stands for as he was uncomprehending of the words of Ambrosius.

At no time in "The Holy Grail" are we really certain that the Cup is anything more than a mirage. If we are to accept Ambrosius and Arthur as the true commentators on the knights' quest—and I feel positive we should—then we find more than a little doubt in their minds about the validity of the vision. Arthur says sceptically at the close of the idyll:

> But if indeed there came a sign from heaven,
> *Blessed are Bors, Lancelot, and Percivale,*
> *For these have seen according to their sight.*
> (ll. 869–871, Roman mine)

Furthermore, the Grail appears to its beholders at such

times and in such ways that we are almost invited to suspect hallucination.

It is characteristic of Tennyson that he makes a woman, Percivale's sister, the first to see the Grail; for in the *Idylls* it is women—Guinevere and Vivien, chiefly among others— who help to destroy men. Moreover, this woman is also a nun; and, as I have attempted to show, to Tennyson the monastic life is an unnatural state which means an unwillingness to accept life and its responsibilities. Percivale informs us that his sister once glowed with "a fervent flame of human love," but that flame "being rudely blunted, glanced and shot / Only to holy things" (ll. 72–76). In other words, she has turned to the ascetic life as compensation for that which was denied her in the world.

In an excess of religious devotion she prays and fasts till, says Percivale,

> *the sun*
> *Shone, and the wind blew, thro' her, and I thought*
> *She might have risen and floated when I saw her.*
>
> (ll. 98–100)

Her religious sense thus stimulated through mortification of the body, the nun is ready for her vision. When the vision does come, it is in almost a state of erotic ecstasy that she perceives it. The similarities between the nun's vision and that of Madeline in Keats's "The Eve of St. Agnes" cannot be overlooked:

> *O never harp nor horn,*
> *Nor aught we blow with breath, or touch with hand,*
> *Was like that music as it came; and then*

Stream'd thro' my cell a cold and silver beam,
And down the long beam stole the Holy Grail,
Rose-red with beatings in it, as if alive,
Till all the white walls of my cell were dyed
With rosy colors leaping on the wall;
And then the music faded, and the Grail
Past, and the beam decay'd, and from the walls
The rosy quiverings died into the night.

(ll. 113–123)

Percivale rushes to Camelot to spread the news that the Grail had reappeared in modern times, and in Galahad especially he finds an eager recipient of this information. Percivale presumably tells his sister about Galahad, and she falls in love with the pure knight because of his religious fervor. She makes a plaited belt of her hair and binds this on him (the Freudian suggestions implicit in this act I leave to my readers to decipher), saying,

My knight, my love, my knight of heaven,
O thou, my love, whose love is one with mine,
I, maiden, round thee, maiden, bind my belt.
Go forth, for thou shalt see what I have seen,
And break thro' all, till one will crown thee king
Far in the spiritual city.

(ll. 157–162)

Percivale informs us that

as she spake
She sent the deathless passion in her eyes
Thro' him, and made him hers, and laid her mind
On him, and he believed in her belief.

(ll. 162–165)

It is clear that, in a manner of speaking, the nun mesmerizes Galahad.

Together the nun and Galahad, along with Percivale no doubt, stir the other knights, in Arthur's absence, up to fever pitch about the Grail. Then one night during a storm, when Galahad is seated in the Siege Perilous hoping to save himself by losing himself, the miracle, at least what passes for a miracle, happens: a dazzling beam of light appears in the hall (is it merely lightning?) and in this light the knights see what they think is the Holy Grail, although it is covered with a "luminous cloud" (which means, probably, that they saw only some smoke from the lightning). The knights look at each other in amazement and are all dumb until Percivale jumps up to swear that *because* he has not seen the Grail he will go in quest of it. Percivale's swearing causes, in turn, the other knights to make the same vow.

When Arthur returns, he is highly sceptical that the knights have indeed seen the Grail. In the verse draft of the idyll Arthur tells them they are following but "A sound, a luminous cloud, a holy nun"; [5] and in the completed poem he asks:

> *'Lo now,' said Arthur, 'have ye seen a cloud?*
> *What go ye into the wilderness to see?'*
>
> (ll. 286–287)

Questioning his knights one by one, he finds that none has seen the Grail save Galahad. Undoubting of the validity of

[5] *Six Tennyson Essays,* p. 162.

Galahad's vision, the King nevertheless says that the sign which he and the nun have seen is "A sign to maim this Order which I made" (l. 297).

The use of the word *maim* here is important, carefully (and ironically) prepared for by the earlier suggestion that the Grail brings health. Percivale had previously told Ambrosius that "if a man / Could touch or see it, he was heal'd at once, / By faith, of all his ills" (ll. 54–56). The nun's confessor had told her that the Grail would "heal the world of all their wickedness" (l. 94); and the nun had told her brother that if the knights saw the vision then might "all the world be heal'd" (l. 128). Arthur, however, recognizes the Grail not as a sign of health and healing but as a sign of disease and destruction. And in the end Arthur is right: the Grail brings death—many of the knights return no more—and, in Lancelot's case, madness.

On their quest the knights, forced to rely on themselves, divorced from the emotional stability offered by Arthur and Camelot, enter a phantasmal world of the imagination where their various identities must be confirmed. In the case of Percivale he is led into a surrealistic wasteland where all is sand and thorns and where all objects of temptation fall into dust. Thirsting for an end to his spiritual unrest, Percivale is first tempted by the beauty of nature as the answer to his search; but when he goes to partake of the apples and the water, they fall into dust. Then follow the temptations of domestic love, earthly glory, and popular applause; but in each case the agents of these temptations fall into dust. For a nature like Percivale's, shut as he is within himself, every fact of life appears phantasmal. It is only when he enters the chapel in the vale, a situation strongly reminiscent of the close of "The Palace of Art," and finds the hermit that he learns why he has been unable to attain the vision he sought. The hermit tells him that he is guilty of pride, mainly of pride in his prowess and his sins. Percivale is, in other words, not properly fit for a spiritual vocation; he has heretofore deluded himself about the potentialities of his own personality; and it is this very lack of spiritual equipment that causes him more or less to go to pieces when thrown into a situation where he must rely only on himself. It is the hermit's function, therefore, to reorient him, to give him a sense of identity. Thus equipped he is better prepared for finding that which he is seeking. Nevertheless, Percivale is unable to find the Grail alone. Only with the help of Galahad, who apparently is of the proper spiritual orientation, does he finally have his glimpse of the Cup—and this only partial and momentary. Percivale is able to transcend his own nature only for an instant, and even this must be accomplished with the aid of someone else.

Tennyson once explained that the key to his subject "is to be found in a careful reading of Sir Percivale's vision and subsequent fall and nineteenth century temptations" (*Memoir*, II, 63). I am not certain what this explanation means—probably it refers to the Oxford Movement—but I do find in these "nineteenth century temptations" something of the temptations which Tennyson as a poet had experienced. Percivale's first hallucinatory experience is described as follows:

> *and when I thought my thirst*
> *Would slay me, saw deep lawns, and then a brook,*
> *With one sharp rapid, where the crisping white*
> *Play'd ever back upon the sloping wave*
> *And took both ear and eye; and o'er the brook*
> *Were apple-trees, and apples by the brook*
> *Fallen, and on the lawns.*

(ll. 379–385)

What could be more like Tennyson's early poetry? But this kind of luxurious, Keatsian poetry of the senses, epitomized in "The Lotus-Eaters," left the poet unsatisfied; and so, prompted by his friends and reviewers, who continually urged upon him a poetry dedicated to more general human experience, Tennyson turned, as I pointed out in the beginning chapter, to the English idylls, to "Dora" and "Edwin Morris," to verse praising the comforts of domestic love. This corresponds to the second temptation which Percivale experiences:

> *And then behold a woman at a door*
> *Spinning; and fair the house whereby she sat.*
> *And kind the woman's eyes and innocent,*
> *And all her bearing gracious; and she rose*
> *Opening her arms to meet me, as who should say,*
> *'Rest here;' but when I touch'd her, lo! she, too,*
> *Fell into dust and nothing, and the house*
> *Became no better than a broken shed,*
> *And in it a dead babe; and also this*
> *Fell into dust, and I was left alone.*

(ll. 391–400)

Percivale's next hallucinatory experience apparently symbolizes the glory of the world especially as it is found in war (ll. 401–420). In Tennyson's poetic development this episode corresponds to his nationalistic verse, such as "The Charge of the Light Brigade," praising England and her battles. Percivale's last mirage symbolizes the inadequacy of fame in man's spiritual life. The knight comes to a walled city on a hill where he finds a great crowd welcoming him and calling him the mightiest and purest among men; but when he reaches the top of the hill he finds the crowd disappeared, only an old man weakly gasping, "Whence and what art thou?" (ll. 421–439). Tennyson himself said that as a young man he had courted fame but that fame had brought him only public "blare and blaze" (*Memoir*, II, 165).

This reading of Percivale's adventures as an allegory of the poet's development may indeed be fanciful, yet in these adventures we find many similarities to the experiences of the speaker in "Merlin and the Gleam," a poem which is admittedly autobiographical. Moreover, when we reflect that it is through Galahad that Percivale is allowed a glimpse of the Grail, we are reminded of Tennyson's dependency on Hallam in *In Memoriam,* where in Lyric CIII it is the "heavenly friend" who indicates the future course of the hitherto aimless poet. In the elegy Hallam becomes, in other words, the agent by whom the speaker is reoriented toward a new "way of the soul." As for Percivale he cannot attain his beatific vision until he identifies himself fully with Galahad:

> *While thus he spake, his eye, dwelling on mine,*
> *Drew me, with power upon me, till I grew*
> *One with him, to believe as he believed.*
>
> (ll. 485–487)

It is Galahad, then, who points the way to the heavenly city just as in *In Memoriam* it is Hallam who points to a new spiritual and poetic way.

If at the beginning of his quest Percivale is totally immersed in self, Bors is, on the other hand, almost too selfless. Pictured on his casque is a pelican, the bird believed to wound its own breast to feed its young. Apparently indifferent to the quest, he vows to undertake the search mainly because his cousin Lancelot does so; and though his love for Lancelot is less destructive than Elaine's, it is nevertheless as unrealistic. For having seen the Grail, he is made sad by the fact that Lancelot did not achieve his clarity of vision. What he wants is not to have this illumination for himself but to see Lancelot healthy. Yet because of his unselfishness, humility, and lack of materialism, he is granted a brief vision of the Holy Cup. He has a "warmth" which, Ambrosius implies, is lacking in many another. In the short but psychologically profound scene upon his return to Camelot, he goes to Lancelot without a word and takes his hand and holds it. When quizzed by Arthur, he is hesitant to admit in front of his recently ill and, so far as he knows, unsuccessful cousin that he has seen the Grail. Bors refuses to speak of his experience and, the narrator tells us, "the tears were in his eyes" (l. 756).

Lancelot undertakes the quest for a burning personal need. He feels corrupted, indeed poisoned, by his sin: in him the wholesome flower and the poisonous flower have grown intertwined; his moral problem has become a psychic problem; and he swears to seek the Grail so that the two flowers

may be plucked asunder. But almost paradoxically he cannot find the Grail until the two are separated; his need
makes success impossible. The quest, therefore, does not heal
or satisfy his need; for instead of separating the flowers and
healing him, the quest leaves the flowers entwined and splits
him apart. His madness returns and he is unmanned,

> beaten down by little men,
> Mean knights, to whom the moving of my sword
> And shadow of my spear had been enow
> To scare them from me once.
>
> (ll. 786–789)

Significantly, his loss of identity occurs when he is away
from Guinevere, on whom he has been so long emotionally
dependent. The account of his quest is taken over almost
wholly from Malory, and I do not therefore think that all
the details of his journey were meant by Tennyson to have
symbolical significance. Nevertheless, Lancelot's flight into
unreality is essentially a voyage into the heart of darkness
where he is left alone with his own defenseless self. His presence in the enchanted towers of Carbonek surrounded by
the sea, a favorite Tennysonian situation, is, I believe, the
self in isolation. Having embarked on the sea to lose himself, he succeeds only in losing his sanity. Yet his very madness, which in Lyric LXXI of *In Memoriam* is identified as
a level of irrational consciousness which admits of visionary
power, is the result of his recognition of the incommensura-
ble elements in his nature; and because of this recognition,
which after all is itself a kind of vision, he is allowed to see

the Grail, although he is not sure about the validity of his vision:

> *And but for all my madness and my sin,*
> *And then my swooning, I had sworn I saw*
> *That which I saw; but what I saw was veil'd*
> *And cover'd. . . .*

(ll. 846–849)

Lancelot is unable to see the Grail with clarity and with sureness of vision because his motive for the quest was not entirely a legitimate one. He seeks for the Cup in order to wash away his sin; he does not want to lose himself to save himself, as did Galahad. When he returns from the quest, consequently, we see that he is no better off—he may perhaps be even worse—than before he set out. He resumes his liaison with Guinevere, falls again into the same old dependency which makes him unable to leave her presence even when he knows it imperative to do so, and lapses again into the double life which he had previously led, the salient moral characteristic of which is betrayal. Quite rightly he concludes, "this quest was not for me" (l. 849).

Galahad is the only one of the knights who is completely successful, for he alone has a religious vocation. Arthur recognizes this fact when he addresses Galahad: "for such / As thou art is the vision, not for these" (ll. 293–294). Unlike the other Grail knights Galahad alone seeks to serve others while on the quest. Not only does he aid Percivale in attaining the vision but also he serves the cause of his King and his God:

> *And in the strength of this [the vision of the Grail] I rode,*
> *Shattering all evil customs everywhere,*
> *And past thro' Pagan realms, and made them mine,*
> *And clash'd with Pagan hordes, and bore them down,*
> *And broke thro' all, and in the strength of this*
> *Come victor.*
>
> (ll. 476–481)

His quest is in no sense an escape or a retreat, as it was for the others. He finds the Grail because his quest is vouchsafed by supernatural agency: a voice cries, "O Galahad, and O Galahad, follow me!" (l. 292). He follows the Grail because he is one of God's chosen, because in fact he can do no other. His exalted spiritual state is signified by the Communion service with Percivale and the hermit: he sees "the fiery face as of a child / That smote itself into the bread and went" (ll. 466–467). The bread for him is not bread but Flesh; for him the spiritual has become the only reality. It doubtlessly was to Galahad, as well as to Arthur's last speech, that Tennyson was referring when he said of "The Holy Grail," "I have expressed there my strong feeling as to the Reality of the Unseen" (*Memoir*, II, 90).

The final comment on the quest, which sets the actions of the Grail knights as well as the nature of their spiritual lives in perspective, is relegated to Arthur. He is not at all diffident about expressing the meaning of the Holy Quest: as far as the ethical life is concerned the result is tragedy. The Round Table decimated, Camelot in ruins, human wrongs left to right themselves, this episode was madness. The Grail knights have been chasing the phantom of a cup that comes and goes, and, except for Galahad, who is lost to the Order, the best vision that any of them had was a fleeting glimpse of the Grail, which so far as their lives are concerned was a meaningless vision. Having sought for a kind of spiritual truth, an abstraction, they failed to realize that truth lacks validity except in so far as man creates it for himself in his actions. Man must not devote his life to this abstraction, says the King, before his work is done, "but, being done, / Let visions of the night or of the day / Come as they will" (ll. 905–907).

Staying at home and accepting his social responsibilities, Arthur too has had visions:

> *and many a time they come,*
> *Until this earth he walks on seems not earth,*
> *This light that strikes his eyeball is not light,*
> *This air that smites his forehead is not air*
> *But vision—yea, his very hand and foot—*
> *In moments when he feels he cannot die,*
> *And knows himself no vision to himself,*
> *Nor the high God a vision, nor that One*
> *Who rose again.*
>
> (ll. 907–911)

But his visions are of such mystical significance as to make the glimpse of a blood-red cup seem inconsequential. While his knights have been chasing wandering fires and at best having fleeting visions, Arthur has remained to do his duty but nevertheless has been rewarded with visions of the most profound sort—visions into the very nature of Absolute Reality.

Arthur's closing speech is, I believe, the key passage to an understanding of "The Holy Grail." Through Arthur's words, Tennyson speaks for the realization of self to be attained through duty and service in the ethical sphere of existence. Man should indeed, says Tennyson here and again in "Merlin and the Gleam," be guided by the gleam; but, the poet insists, the gleam hovers over the world, touching on man and his works. Not until the end of life does it point heavenwards, when, says Arthur, man's work is done. For only when man has served his fellows is he fully prepared to serve God. Love and duty—these are the basic principles of man's life; and all which tends to pervert or obscure these principles should, Tennyson implies in "The Holy Grail," be condemned as harmful and pernicious.

VII

"Balin and Balan": Mark's way

Hallam Tennyson tells that with the publication of "Gareth and Lynette" in 1872 his father thought he had completed the cycle of the *Idylls of the King* but later felt some further introduction to "Merlin and Vivien" was necessary, and so wrote "Balin and Balan." To be sure, Vivien does make her first appearance in "Balin and Balan"; but since we see her as the same malevolent figure as in "Merlin and Vivien," how does her appearance here serve to elucidate "Merlin and Vivien"? The answer to the question lies, I think, not so much in the introduction of Vivien herself as in the introduction of King Mark.

We first meet Mark in "Gareth and Lynette." A vassal king, Mark sends a present to King Arthur, asking to be made a member of the Round Table. Arthur rejects the gift, calling Mark

> *a man of plots,*
> *Craft, poisonous counsels, wayside ambushings—*
> *. . . who strikes nor lets the hand be seen.*

(ll. 423–427)

He next appears in "Balin and Balan," where Vivien is de-scribed as "one from out the hall of Mark" (l. 431). His third appearance is in "Merlin and Vivien," where he conspires with Vivien to corrupt Arthur's court from within. Lastly Mark appears in "The Last Tournament" as the treacherous slayer of Tristram. Sneaking up on the lovers from behind, he cleaves Tristram through the brain; this is "Mark's way" (l. 748).

From the various references to Mark we see that he is asso-ciated with malice, particularly with treachery. Further-more, we see that he is allied with Vivien, who likewise seems to be a representation of malice. But what is the motivation for their malevolence? Tennyson does not pro-vide the answer. He seems to see evil as a presence which forever lurks in the background, working its harm without cause, always ready to strike when it finds an opening. Its means of action, Tennyson implies, is through disloyalty and slander. As embodiments of evil, both Mark and Vivien are antitheses to Arthur, who lives by the maxim "Man's word is God in man." In "Balin and Balan" Tennyson pre-sents an example of how the forces such as Mark and Vivien exemplify can destroy both the individual and society. The idyll is, in fact, an exemplum on the text "Man's word is God in man."

Like nearly all the other characters in *Idylls of the King,* Balin is morbidly dependent on someone else. By himself Balin is but half a man. The very type of the headstrong, impulsive man, Balin requires Balan, his calm and rational twin, to complete his nature. Balan is, in other words, his balance; without him Balin is subject to all the violences of the Prince in *The Princess* when he too is but half a man. This means that Balin is especially susceptible to slander and other forms of treachery, to taking the true for false and the false for true.

Formerly when he had been at Camelot without his brother, Balin had been banished from the court because he half slew one of Arthur's men who "had spoken evil of me" (l. 56). He is now readmitted to the Order with the help of Balan, who during the three years of exile from the court has made Balin, nicknamed "the Savage," less wild; with Balan present he moves in harmony with the Order and the King.

Soon, however, the envoys sent to Pellam to collect his due tribute return with the information that in the woods surrounding Pellam's castle there is a monster which kills foully and villainously and which recently has slain one of Arthur's knights. They report that a woodsman has told them that this demon

> Was once a man, who, driven by evil tongues
> From all his fellows, lived alone, and came
> To learn black magic, and to hate his kind
> With such a hate that when he died his soul
> Became a fiend, which, as the man in life
> Was wounded by blind tongues he saw not whence,
> Strikes from behind.

(ll. 122–128)

In this transparent reference to slander we are reminded of Arthur's description of Mark in "Gareth and Lynette" as one "who strikes nor lets the hand be seen."

To track this monster down is the allotted quest of Balan. But Balan is apprehensive about the welfare of his brother if left alone; and he warns his twin to "hold them outer fiends, / Who leap at thee to tear thee" (ll. 138–139), which words I again understand as a reference to slander. So advised, Balin realizes that he is not yet self-sufficient: he needs something or someone to take the place of Balan. He decides to ask for permission to bear the Queen's crown-royal on his shield, "In lieu of this rough beast upon my shield, / Langued gules, and tooth'd with grinning savagery" (ll. 192–193). If I follow the allegorical drift correctly, this indicates that by means of the emblem, supposedly signifying all that is best in Camelot, he will lay the fiend slander with its lying red tongues.

But Balin unhappily chooses the wrong emblem for emotional support. He looks not to the King—that is, the ideal man—but to Lancelot and Guinevere as models to imitate. Arthur says: "The crown is but the shadow of the king, / And this a shadow's shadow . . ." (ll. 199–200). Balin not only makes the mistake of taking false for true but also attempts, more or less in the manner of Pellam, to feed a pining life by playing with symbols. When Balin's models prove imperfect, he has no means for sustaining his psychic equilibrium.

Having with the aid of his new emotional prop momentarily conquered his penchant to believe the worst, he resists an inclination toward violence when he fancies he sees the thrall he almost slew smile at him. But having taken Guinevere and Lancelot as his models, and not realizing, as the King has told him, that the emblem on his shield is but "a shadow's shadow" of the King, he is emotionally defenseless when he sees his emblem about to be sullied. Hitherto too prompt to believe any evil he hears, he now is unwilling to believe what he sees. "I see not what I see," he says to himself after having watched the tryst between Lancelot and Guinevere, and "hear not what I hear" (ll. 276–277). In a mad frenzy he flees from Camelot.

Balin follows the same track as that followed by Balan, and in the woods he meets a churl who tells him about the demon of the wood. Balin replies, "To lay that devil would lay the devil in me" (l. 296); he wrongly thinks the overthrow of slander would diminish his own tendency to believe the worst. As he rides on he passes the cave "Whereout the demon issued up from hell" (l. 312), yet he marks not that slander comes from hell.

At Pellam's court the vassal king's son, Garlon, who also is reputed to ride unseen throughout the woods, hints at Guinevere's illicit affair with Lancelot. Remembering the crown on his shield, Balin is able to restrain himself upon the first occasion; but when next day Garlon again insults the emblem of the Queen, the prop which supports Balin's sanity, he fells Garlon with his sword, crying, "So thou be shadow, here I make thee ghost" (l. 388). He does not comprehend that his own credulity of ill must be overthrown before the monster slander can be slain.

After the murder he feels unworthy of the quite unrealistic ideal he has of the Queen, and so, determined to carry it no longer, he hangs the shield on a tree. At this point

Vivien, the damsel-errant from Mark's court, appears to tell him her lies about the Queen. Believing her, he feels his evil spirit leap upon him, and he destroys his shield, a symbol of his ideal at Camelot. He lets out a weird yell "Unearthlier than all shriek of bird or beast" (l. 536), which Balan hearing recognizes as the scream of the wood-devil he came to quell. In accepting the lies of Vivien, Balin has become infected by slander, has become, in fact, the demon himself.

Balin's is but one instance of madness among the knights of the Round Table; the other two instances are those of Lancelot and Pelleas. In each case Tennyson characterizes insanity by means of animal imagery. Originally identified by a beast on his shield, Balin rushes off to the forest after overseeing the meeting between Lancelot and Guinevere. Here we are told that he, "blind and deaf to all / Save that chain'd rage which ever yelpt within, / Past eastward from the falling sun" (ll. 313–315). Retreating to the heart of darkness, Balin feels his madness crying like a wild beast from within. Moreover, he speaks to Vivien in a striking animal image:

> *Here I dwell*
> *Savage among the savage woods, here die—*
> *Die—let the wolves' black maws ensepulchre*
> *Their brother beast, whose anger was his lord.*
>
> (ll. 478–481)

Finally, there is Balin's beastlike yell and Vivien's last remark, "Leave them to the wolves" (l. 577).

Lancelot is obsessed by lions. When he meets Bors on his

quest for the Grail, he tells that "there is a lion in the way" ("The Holy Grail," l. 643). (Significantly, the shield of Lancelot bears lions on an azure field.) Then in his madness, the interior journey into the palace of Carbonek, he passes rampant lions at the sea gate which almost destroy him. As for Pelleas, after his betrayal by Gawain he becomes a beast as well as a fool and in his mad rage sees Camelot as a "Black nest of rats" ("Pelleas and Ettarre," l. 544). The world becomes for him a place of snakes, foxes, wolves, and rats.

It should be noted that for each of the three knights madness results from the loss of an emotional prop: Balin's occurs when he loses Balan and the shield, Lancelot's when he is separated from Guinevere, Pelleas' when he is betrayed by Gawain and loses Ettarre. Sanity returns only when the prop is restored; if the emotional support is not regained, as in the case of Pelleas, the mental damage is permanent.

It should be further noted that each man when mad withdraws into a wilderness—Balin into the forest, Lancelot into a wasteland, Pelleas into a rocky landscape. With great skill Tennyson uses the landscape to mirror the emotional and mental condition of each knight. The setting in "Balin and Balan" is especially interesting. In this interior landscape the woods becomes an analogue of Balin's mind. It is characterized by confusion and deceit and is inhabited by a fiend; it is, in other words, Balin himself.

Another striking series of images associated with sanity is that of music. In the beginning of "Balin and Balan" the two brothers sit beside the "carolling water" (l. 42). For-

merly when Balin had been at Camelot without his brother
he had been given an "unmelodious name"—"the Savage"
(ll. 50–51)—but now with the aid of his twin and the emblem
on his shield he "felt his being move / In music with his
Order and the King" (ll. 207–208). Here music is equated
with sanity and social order while silence is associated with
anger, madness, and disorder:

> *The nightingale, full-toned in middle May,*
> *Hath ever and anon a note so thin*
> *It seems another voice in other groves;*
> *Thus, after some quick burst of sudden wrath,*
> *The music in him seem'd to change and grow*
> *Faint and far-off.*
>
> (ll. 209–214)

When Vivien appears on the scene she dumbs "the wholesome music of the wood" (l. 430) and with her lies she dis-
rupts the inner harmony within Balin and elicits from him
the unearthly shriek of the madman.

Ironically the person whom Balin elects to fight is the one
person who could help him regain his former state of equilibrium—Balan. The lie, a violation of Arthur's dictum that
"Man's word is God in man," has served to destroy. Balin
and Balan, whom we now see as one double self, can exist
only when in harmony one with the other. When by means
of insidious evil such as slander the self is divided, then self-
destruction is the result; the better as well as the baser nature is lost to the world. "We two were born together," says
Balan, "and we die / Together by one doom" (ll. 617–618).

After the fight Balan, now rejoined with Balin, does restore his brother to a state of balance. Not only does he present himself as the old prop who helps abate Balin's credulousness of evil, but he also restores to Balin the prop of his ideal, the Queen. "Pure as our own true mother is our Queen" (l. 606), he assures his brother. As for Vivien, she is the playmate of Garlon:

> 'She dwells among the woods,' he said, 'and meets
> And dallies with him in the Mouth of Hell.'
>
> (ll. 603–604)

At the end, therefore, Balin has both his supports, is completely sane and balanced; but now, near death, his props can be of no avail. The rough beast with langued gules, the original device on Balin's shield, has conquered.

Vivien and Garlon are the agents of the beast; and proper agents they are, for each, a destructive instrument, is a child of death. Garlon is, of course, the son of Pellam, who in his religious fanaticism has denied life. Eating scarcely enough to keep his pulse beating, having cast off his wife and refused to let women enter his gates, he spends his days locked up with bones of martyrs, thorns of the Crown, slivers of the Cross, and the spear that pierced Christ's side—all of them associated with death. "I have quite foregone / All matter of this world," he says (ll. 113–114). His castle is a "ruinous donjon" hidden from the sun; no light or life is admitted:

> Leaves
> Laid their green faces flat against the panes,
> Sprays grated, and the canker'd boughs without
> Whined in the wood; for all was hush'd within. . . .
>
> (ll. 338–341)

The castle is in fact a grave, appearing "as a knoll of moss, /
The battlement overtopt with ivy-tods, / A home of bats, in
every tower an owl" (ll. 329–331). This is the perfect setting
for Pellam, who is the embodiment of death-in-life.

Vivien also, as was pointed out in another chapter, is a
child of death. Her father too was an enemy of the King. She
tells Mark:

> *My father died in battle against the King,*
> *My mother on his corpse in open field;*
> *She bore me there, for born from death was I*
> *Among the dead and sown upon the wind—*
> *And then on thee!*
>
> ("Merlin and Vivien," ll. 42–46)

Her patron has been the dastard King of Cornwall, and with
him she has learned "That old true filth, and bottom of the
well / Where Truth is hidden" ("Merlin and Vivien," ll. 47–
48). When she enters the *Idylls,* she comes as the emissary of
Mark.

Neither Garlon nor Vivien can believe in purity, for they
cannot understand what is above them. Denying the life of
the spirit and believing only in material force, they can only
comprehend animal lust, and so they see the world only in
terms of themselves. It is for this reason that Garlon attempts
to sully the emblem of the crown which Balin carries and
that Vivien believes of Balin that "This fellow hath wrought
some foulness with his Queen; / Else never had he borne
her crown, nor raved / And thus foam'd over at a rival
name" (ll. 556–558). Thus limited by their own predilec-

tions for ill, the agents of evil likewise mistake the true for false.

"Balin and Balan" is a masterful interweaving of the main themes of the *Idylls of the King*. The last published, "Balin and Balan" was Tennyson's last opportunity to weave threads of continuity to tie together the episodic structure of the *Idylls*. Here indeed we find those themes—false vision, emotional dependency, asceticism and religious enthusiasm, treachery and betrayal—which provide the core of meaning to the *Idylls*. Significantly, "Balin and Balan" is the first idyll to have an unhappy ending.

If "Merlin and Vivien" is "Vivien's way," then is "Balin and Balan" "Mark's way." While Vivien, as we have seen, works as an active force of evil, Mark works insidiously. Not actually an actor in the idyll, Mark nevertheless hovers in the background as the source from which evil springs. This explains why he is ultimately responsible for the tragedy of Balin: like Mark, slander never shows its face, but it wreaks its havoc effectively all the same.

VIII

A new realism

When we consider the large part that disguise plays in the *Idylls,* when we reflect on the numerous instances of false vision, when we remember Tennyson's explanation of the meaning of his poem as "the dream of man coming into practical life" (*Memoir,* II, 127), we must conclude that illusion is a major theme of the work. At least three times in the poem itself Tennyson points to the overriding importance of this theme. In the first of the idylls of "The Round Table," Merlin, like Hans Sachs in *Die Meistersinger,* declares that all is "Confusion, and illusion, and relation, / Elusion, and occasion, and evasion" ("Gareth and Lynette," ll. 281–282). *In propria persona* the author begins "Geraint and Enid" by describing earthly existence as "the feeble twilight" in which the "purblind race of miserable men" grope about "taking true for false, or false for true." Dagonet, the Fool, speaks of the illusory nature of existence by describing, first, the world as "flesh and shadow" and, secondly, Arthur's great illusion in thinking that "he can make / Figs out of thistles, silk from bristles, milk / From burning spurge, honey from hornet-combs, / And men from beasts" ("The Last Tournament," ll. 315–316, 355–358).

Almost all the actors in the *Idylls* are, in one way or another, victims of their illusions. Lynette thinks Gareth a kitchen knave, Geraint believes Enid false, Balin accepts Lancelot and Guinevere as worthy models, Merlin blinds himself to the snares of Vivien, Elaine lives in fantasy, the Grail knights follow wandering fires, Pelleas convinces himself that Ettarre loves him, Tristram and Isolt seek salvation in erotic passion, Guinevere is blinded to the greatness of the King, Bedivere is deluded by material values. Each of them does not or cannot see reality for what it is—and so because of their impercipiency they fail. And in their failure they help to bring about the failure of the King. For their transgressions deny the validity of the King's great illusion —namely, that he can create a perfect society.

Arthur comes into the world a simple man; in fact, he says so himself: "For I, being simple, thought to work His will" ("The Passing of Arthur," l. 22). He had thought to create a perfect society by creating perfect men. He bound his knights to vows of perfection. But he did this without taking into account the nature of men. Quite rightly then does Dagonet, a Fool himself, call Arthur the king of fools. For Arthur cannot see things as they are, does not perceive the resistance of reality to human desire and will. Only at the end does he comprehend the impossibility of his ideal, because only then is he made aware of the paradox of reality.

To make men perfect, he must mold them as he would have them be. But in attempting to make them perfect, he must demand the submission of their wills to his, thus denying to them their own individualities. The moral indefensibility of his position eventually becomes plain. Yet if he permits his knights to act in a way other than that he has enjoined, his plan for a perfect society can never be fulfilled. So in the end Arthur is brought face to face with this paradox: to be morally responsible, power must be self-limiting—that is, it must allow the freedom of the individual will; but limited power is a contradiction and, moreover, does not allow the successful accomplishment of that which power desires.

Arthur's dilemma is almost precisely that of Wotan's in *The Ring of the Nibelung*. In a remarkable instance of cultural convergence Wagner addresses himself in the *Ring* to the same problem which preoccupies Tennyson in the *Idylls*. Like Arthur, Wotan is motivated by the desire to found for man a satisfactory society and, again like Arthur, finds his desire frustrated by the nature of reality. To attain his goal he must win from Alberich the gold stolen from the Rhine Maidens; yet this can only be achieved by thievery and trickery, in effect causing Wotan to violate the laws which he himself has established and which sustain his power. As Erda warns him, he must either give up the ring or lose his power; but, Erda continues, even if he does return the ring, he will lose his power anyway. The problem is insoluble; the paradox cannot be resolved. And Wotan and Valhalla fade away just as do Arthur and Camelot, and only at the final hour comes the stripping away of illusion. Wagner's point is the same as Tennyson's: the hero cannot redeem the world because the world is irredeemable.

On Tennyson's part this represents a darkening of the vision of the world presented in *In Memoriam,* in fact a reversal of the ideas set forth therein. Where *In Memoriam* postulates the perfect man resulting from evolutionary progress, *Idylls of the King* denies progress of almost every sort. For the *Idylls* says that in this world separated from the true reality of the eternal deep by enshrouding mists, appearance is mistaken for reality. Confusion and illusion are, as Merlin states, inevitable, and the result is not moral evolution but moral failure.

But what of the man who is able to pierce the veil of appearances and see things as they are? Tennyson anticipates the question by showing what happens to the man without illusions. In the case of Merlin the result is despair and, finally, death. Alone of the inhabitants of Camelot, Merlin recognizes Vivien for the evil creature that she is and for the evil which she represents. He knows that evil is soon to overcome Camelot, is soon indeed to assault even himself. Yet in spite of his knowledge, he is powerless to make defense against it; for human as he is—and thus subject to illusion—he deludes himself finally that Vivien is not what he knows her to be and so resigns his will to hers. Existence without illusion is too dreadful to endure. Tennyson knew as well as Eliot that humankind cannot bear very much reality.

In the case of Dagonet, the Fool, the knowledge of truth

is likewise immobilizing. He has learned that the world is not as it seems and that man can never understand it:

> *I have wallow'd, I have wash'd—the world*
> *Is flesh and shadow—I have had my day.*
> *The dirty nurse, Experience, in her kind*
> *Hath foul'd me—an I wallow'd, then I wash'd—*
> *I have had my day and my philosophies—*
> *And thank the Lord I am King Arthur's fool.*
>
> ("The Last Tournament," ll. 314–320)

Unlike every other actor in the *Idylls* except Merlin, Dagonet seems to realize that the opposites and antinomies of the world can never be reconciled, and knowing this he seems to accept the irreducible polarities of existence. Life is a set of illusions, and without these illusions man has nothing to work with. Thus Arthur with his ideals is the king of fools, but better Arthur with his illusions than a king without them: "Long live the king of fools." Yet at the end Dagonet, like Merlin, cannot endure without some illusions to live by. Seeing the inevitable soon to occur, Dagonet tells Arthur at the close of "The Last Tournament," "And I shall never make thee smile again."

In the last of the *Idylls* Arthur too learns that life is made up of illusions: "eyes of men are dense and dim, / And have not power to see it [the world] as it is." And he apprehends that his also has been an endeavor based on illusions: he had thought to work to the enrichment of the world, but "all whereon I lean'd . . . / Is traitor to my peace, and all my realm / Reels back into the beast, and is no more" (ll. 19–26). Yet he penetrates to this perception only in his final moments; and having learned, he must pass on. His confusion stemming from this discovery makes him unable to continue. "O Bedivere," he cries out, "for on my heart hath fallen / Confusion, till I know not what I am, / Nor whence I am, nor whether I be king; / Behold, I seem but king among the dead" (ll. 143–146). Life without illusions is impossible; the will can be gratified only when the world of man ceases to exist.

The *Idylls,* then, denies the progressionism of *In Memoriam* and sets forth a new ontology. In place of the brave new world offered in the elegy, the *Idylls* presents a world of near absurdity, a world perhaps with a plan but whose teleology is undecipherable. "O me!" Arthur cries out in question, "for why is all around us here / As if some lesser god had made the world, / But had not force to shape it as he would . . . ?" ("The Passing of Arthur," ll. 12–14). What is tragic about existence is that the possibility of love and freedom and beauty can never be seized. God made the world and His handiwork is evident. "I found Him in the shining of the stars, / I mark'd Him in the flowering of His fields," Arthur says, "But in His ways with men I find Him not" ("The Passing of Arthur," ll. 9–11). This is in marked contradiction to the closing lyrics of *In Memoriam,* wherein the speaker declares, "I found Him not in world or sun" (Lyric CXXIV). No longer disturbed by biological evolution, Tennyson turns his attention to moral evolution and enunciates his doubt about the possibility of such progress.

In the *Idylls* Tennyson suggests that in their relations

with other human beings men can never achieve mutual recognition of each other's freedom because it is impossible for them to treat other persons as ends. He shows this, I believe, not only in the character of Arthur but also in the lovers who use each other as means to satisfy desire. This view led him to the conclusion that the essence of relations between conscious beings is not community and mutuality but conflict. It is important to remember that among the major actors in the *Idylls* there is not one example of full mutual understanding between two characters. (Perhaps Balin and Balan may be argued as exceptions, but they are, if I understand Tennyson's intention correctly, to be regarded as dual aspects of one individual.) This is not to say, of course, that love is not the desired end; rather, it is to say that love in the sense of complete sympathy and understanding is impossible because of the nature of existence itself.

Faced with a world characterized by illusions and governed by conflict, what is man to do? Is he to retreat from action into speculation or is he to act "naturally" on his perception that conflict is the law of life? To both possibilities Tennyson in the *Idylls* offers an emphatic no. He leaves us with no doubt that Percivale's way and the Red Knight's way are to be abhorred. What man must do is act as though love were the great cosmological principle, which means that he must commit himself to an ethical existence; in other words, man must delude himself that he is adding to the sum of perfection in the world—this in spite of the fact that retrogression is the concomitant of progress. This is, I think, what Merlin means when he tells Gareth that the King "Will bind thee by such vows as is a shame / A man should not be bound by, yet the which / No man can keep" ("Gareth and Lynette," ll. 266–268); and it is also what Dagonet means when he praises Arthur as the king of fools.

In exemplifying the paradoxical nature of existence Tennyson was not turning his back on theism. Throughout the *Idylls* he makes clear his hero's belief in God. Above all, Tennyson affirms that the self can rest only upon God and discover itself in its eternal qualities only through God. With Kierkegaard, he would agree that the only authentic existence is that which is "before God," and would insist that all science, philosophy, morals, and politics must take into consideration human destiny and all the historical conditions of that destiny—Original Sin and Redemption. At the end of the *Idylls* his Arthur may have doubts about Christian faith—for example, Arthur tells Bedivere, "For all my mind is clouded with a doubt" ("The Passing of Arthur," l. 426)—but Arthur becomes a hero of faith only when he is subject to uneasiness and doubt. Now in his confusion and anxiety he transcends his old self as an ethically oriented individual and assumes a new and (Tennyson would have us believe) higher self—the self confronting the infinite. The path to faith is thus prepared by doubt, which marks the defeat of reason.

Much of the *Idylls* appears to be the expression of a pessimistic philosophy. Friends and wife prove untrue, and the last great battle in the west results in the destruction of all that is high and holy. Nevertheless, at the end the new sun rises bringing a new year; there is hope in the new day. Moreover, though systems and governments may fail, Tennyson tells in the Epilogue "To the Queen," "The goal of this great world / Lies beyond sight." Faith, therefore, is not only belief in mysteries above reason but also hope justified by no rational reason.

Tennyson's vision in *Idylls of the King* is ultimately Christian. Everything he is recorded as saying about his poem points to this conclusion. Whether it is orthodoxly Christian is another matter and one which should not concern us overmuch, for the great tenets of Christian faith— Original Sin and Redemption—are implicit. More specifically, his vision here is that of the Christian existentialist, thus a vision different from that reflected in *In Memoriam*. The elegy deals with the search for truth by means of speculation on and contemplation of the transcendental world, and it gives a picture of man knowing himself through transcendental experience. The *Idylls*, however, shows man achieving value through encounter with earthly experience and, further, portrays, especially in "The Holy Grail," the inadequacy of transcendental experience as a guide to conduct. Tennyson is clear that there is no truth for the individual except in so far as he creates it for himself in his actions. Hence the necessity for self-committal and unswerving performance in the demands of that commitment. In contradiction to *In Memoriam* the *Idylls* implies that reality as a thought is never more than a possibility, whereas life properly conceived is concerned only with the instant, which is reality itself. Let us recall what Tennyson himself said, "Birth is a mystery and death is a mystery, and in the midst lies the tableland of life, and its struggles and performances" (*Memoir*, II, 127).

In the *Idylls* Tennyson takes into account all the contradictions of existence. For the poem represents existence as blossoming in eternity but accomplished in the instant; it portrays that existence as choice and expectation, risk and gain, life and death, the past declaring itself in the present; and finally it shows life as a permanent tension between the finite and the infinite. The philosophy of the *Idylls* is thus a realism, and as such a reversal of the transcendentalism of *In Memoriam*.

Idylls of the King should be regarded as Tennyson's *magnum opus*. Shaped and reshaped over a period of many years, it is the artistic embodiment of Tennyson's most mature thought. With what the poet called its "parabolic drift" (*Memoir*, II, 127) it interweaves numerous themes, so that the poem as a whole contains many layers of meaning, a few of which have been touched on here. It is their co-existence and interplay that make the *Idylls of the King* a poem of which one never tires.

Index